DRY THOSE TEARS

Robert A. Russell

ISBN: 978-1-63923-499-8

Printed: November 2022

Cover Art By: Amit Paul

Published and Distributed By:
Lushena Books
607 Country Club Drive, Unit E
Bensenville, IL 60106
www.lushenabks.com

ISBN: 978-1-63923-499-8

DRY THOSE TEARS

Robert A. Russell

Contents

If you would indeed behold the spirit of death, open your heart wide unto the body of life.

For life and death are one, even as the river and sea are one.

KAHLIL GIBRAN

CHAPTER 1

A Letter

Dear Friend,

Losing a dear one by death is one of the most difficult experiences you will ever be called upon to go through. When death takes from you some one whom you loved dearly, your life immediately seems empty and forlorn. Your heart is broken, and you can see nothing more to live for. You reach for a hand that has vanished, and you listen for a voice that is still.

It is natural to grieve at such a time, but it is unnatural to capitulate to grief. The difference between controlled and uncontrolled grief depends largely upon the degree of one's religious faith.

I have seen all kinds of people in all kinds of sorrow over a long period of years. Some are comforted and transfigured in their grief, and others are torn to pieces by it. Why? Because some have a faith and understanding equal to their need, and others do not. Some have access to the Divine Presence, and others shut themselves out. Of course, I sympathize with you in your sorrow, but I want to do something more than sympathize. I want to bring you comfort, healing, and peace. Others have found consolation and release in times like these, and this comfort is available to you too, It is just a matter of facing the facts about your loss and of seeing things as they are.

What are the facts? One: Your loved one has made his change; so you must face your loss. Two: Death is inevitable; so you must accept it. Three: Death is only an appearance; so you must get behind it.

What do we mean by facing your loss? James Gilkey records two contrasting stories that well illustrate this point.

"Recently an American mother received word from the War Department that her only son had been killed. . . . Subsequently, the fact of his death was confirmed, and all possibility of a mistake in identification was eliminated. Yet the boy's mother stubbornly refused to face the fact that her boy was dead. She continued to center all her conversation on him and his return. She re-papered and re-furnished her entire house, explaining that her son had never liked the dwelling and that now it must please him. Then she began collecting clippings and cartoons which she thought would interest him, past-ing them in scrapbooks and stacking the scrapbooks in his room. They would be waiting there when he returned! What was the meaning of these strange actions? The boy's mother was refusing to face her loss; she was denying her grief its normal outlet; she was trying to escape suffering by pretending that the occasion for pain did not exist."*

Analyze her attitude and you will see that she was not meeting her problem but complicating it. She was living in a make-believe world. Her denial of her grief was like confining steam in a boiler with no valves. In other words, she was delaying her grief; and by the delay, she was multiplying it.

In contrast to the story of the mother who refused to face her loss is the story of Mrs. Jacob Walker who, for years, kept the lighthouse on Robbins Reef between New York Harbor and Manhattan Island. Here is the story as she told it.

"I was a young girl living at Sandy Hook, New Jersey, when I first met my husband. He was the keeper of the Sandy Hook Light, and took me there as his bride. I was happy there, for the lighthouse was on land and I could have a garden and raise flowers. Then one day we were transferred here — to

*Ina May Greer

Robbins Reef. As soon as we arrived, I said to my husband, 'I can't stay here! The sight of water wherever I look makes me too lonesome. I won't unpack.'

"But somehow all the trunks and boxes got unpacked. Four years later my husband caught a heavy cold while tending the light. The cold turned into pneumonia, and they took him to the Infirmary on Staten Island where he could have better care than I could give him here. I stayed behind to tend the light in his place. A few nights later, I saw a rowboat coming through the darkness. Something told me the message it was bringing. Even before the man in the boat spoke, I knew what he would say. 'We're sorry, but your husband's worse.' 'You mean he's dead,' I answered; and there was no reply. We buried my husband on Staten Island. Every morning when the sun comes up, I stand at that porthole and look in the direction of his grave. Sometimes the hill is green, sometimes it is brown, sometimes it is white with snow. But it always brings a message from him — something I heard him say more often than anything else. Just three words — 'Mind the light!' "

After you have faced the fact of your loss, accept it; that is, resign yourself to it. Since death is one of life's inevitables, there is nothing we can do to change it. It must be accepted with courage, faith, and understanding. How can you do that? By deliberately picking up your life and going on.

The third thing you must do is to get behind your loss. See your departed love as he is in his new life. Up till now you have been thinking of him as dead. You have been concerned about his present condition. You have been wondering where he is and if he is all right. Now you must establish a new relationship to him by getting behind the appearance of death.

This new relationship will come in the Silence. Jesus said, *"I go to prepare a place for you, that where I am, there ye may be also."* Where is this place? It is within you and within every individual. It is a holy place, prepared by Christ in consciousness.

Stillness fills this place. The Peace of God is in it. Your loved one is in it. When you enter there, the world outside, your griefs, and your fears drop away, and you rise at last with new comfort, vision, and understanding. This place is not in a church or in a sequestered spot surrounded by high walls and guarded by locked doors. It is within you and all about you whenever you silence the material senses and go alone with God.

Clifford Harrison speaks for the one who has gone on:

I am in your thought, Oh! seek for me there!
I move in your memories, breathe in your prayer!
I am yours as I never was yours before;
You are mine as you never were mine of yore.

Right now I want you to sit down in some quiet place, and let me speak to you from the pages of this book. Assume a comfortable position, close your eyes, and relax yourself into God. Say quietly to yourself, *"Underneath are the everlasting arms."* Then relax your body; still your feeling and your thought. Feel the Presence of God freeing you from every shackle of grief, sorrow, and fear. Get the peace of God into every atom of your being. Become so still that the God within you is one with the God above you. Let your relaxation be so complete that each cell of your body becomes conscious of its Source.

"The Lord is in his holy temple [you]. *Let all the earth* [your body, every nerve, every cell, every muscle] *keep silent before Him."* Lean back upon God, and rest relaxed within a pervading sense of Divine Life, Power, and Peace. Whenever you feel any tension of grief, relax your mind and let go.

Meet intrusion or suggestion of your loss with Whittier's lines:

> . . . Life is ever Lord of Death,
> And Love can never lose its own.

Hold yourself in this relaxed state of mind until you feel a sense of God's Presence enveloping all the earth—yourself, your family, your friends, everyone—with everlasting peace and understanding. If you are disturbed at any moment during this period by your grief or your problem, repeat the words: *"Underneath are the everlasting arms."* Then relax once more gently into God. Keep doing this until you no longer think about nor feel your loss.

Fix your attention upon the truth of St. Paul's words, *"In Him we live, and move, and have our being."* This statement means that there is but One Mind, and that we are all in It. You are in It, and your loved one is in It. It is our means of communication, both in the physical body and out of it. This One Mind is everywhere equally present. It is wherever we are. Your mind and your loved one's mind are just parts of the One Mind, and they are as close to each other at this moment as they ever were. Since there is only One Mind and we are all in It, nothing can sever our communication.

As we reflect that our Christ Self — Real Self — is in God's Mind now, and that the Christ, or Spiritual Being of our loved one is also in that Mind, we shall have an unmistakable sense of communication. It will come either as a detailed message or, as is more often the case, as a deep impression that we have been with him and he has been with us.

This is not spiritualism, but the Truth of Being which is in accord with Jesus' statement to His disciples, *"I go away and come again unto you." "God is Spirit"* and *"ye are Spirit."* Spiritual things are spiritually discerned. Your loved ones are as much with you as your consciousness; but if you believe them to be dead, then they are dead within yourself, and communication with them is impossible.

I hope you will read on. I have gathered together in these pages the best thinking that I have found in literature on the subject of death and have recorded the conclusions I have come to after long thought and long service to others, to the end that your heart will be comforted, your thought stimulated, your faith revived, and that experiencing the nearness of death will leave you a better, finer, more understanding person.

Sincerely yours,
Robert A. Russell

CHAPTER 2

Grief

The death of a loved one is a heart-shattering experience, not because of his transition to a fuller and more complete life, but because of our sense of separation, loneliness, and loss. One day he is with us in the flesh; the next day he is gone. Grief is the most distressing of all human problems because nothing on the material plane can lessen it. The solution lies in a complete catharsis, or clarification.

One of our difficulties is that we are unprepared when sorrow comes. We buy life insurance and we make wills, but we do not protect ourselves against the shock of grief. We are like the farmer who puts lightning rods on his barn after the lightning strikes. It is in the time of our strength, health, and happiness that we must prepare for sorrow.

But when life moves along serenely and smoothly, the necessity of preparing for bereavement does not occur to us. Yet there is nothing more certain in human life. Sorrow is inevitable, and we should prepare for it just as we prepare for college or old age. We should prepare for it by building within ourselves a deep faith in the unity and continuity of all life.

Those who prepare for sorrow suffer infinitely less than those who do not. A certain minister, on the day after the funeral of his only son, filled the speaking engagements which were a part of his duties. His friends said to him: "How can you carry on so soon after the death of your son?" Note his reply: "Years ago, my wife and I talked these things over. We reasoned that life would not always be sweet, that life would not always be pleasant. We knew that there would be dark and bleak days when seemingly not a ray of light would be seen. We decided that in the days of our freedom from sorrow we would build into our lives enough faith, hope, confidence, and trust in God to give us something on which to stand when sorrow came upon us." It was the power resulting from that decision which upheld him in the loss of his child.

Uncontrolled grief is one of the most injurious emotions in human life. It will not only destroy health and impair efficiency, but will also bring poverty. Socrates says: "He that grieves much is a magnet to attract waste of property." Those who give way to grief often suffer not only the loss of material possessions and health but other negative ills as well. Does that sound like an exaggeration?

Then ask those who have become confirmed invalids through grief. Ask the arthritic and rheumatic patients. They are often the people who were unprepared for sorrow. When death came, they were overwhelmed by it. They had nothing to stand on—nothing to bear them up. If you cannot rise above sorrow when it comes, you lay yourself open to the waste and disintegration which it brings.

Have you ever analyzed grief? Then do so now. Grief is a negative emotion, and like other emotions, it demands expression. It cannot be suppressed, destroyed, denied, or delayed. The person who stoically refused to express his grief only complicates it. He pushes it down into the subconscious mind where it gathers power like steam confined in a boiler. Unexpressed grief results in shattered nerves. Disposing of all the personal effects of a loved one does not solve the problem of sorrow any more than refusing to think about him does.

Emotion not only demands expression; it demands action. It must be dealt with scientifically and spiritually. It is a force with which we must do something; fortunately it can be sublimated, that is, turned to a constructive purpose.

We can use it to deepen faith, expand vision, and to recreate and enrich life. We can use it to make the lives of others happier and more complete. Yes, I know. This is easier said than done, but there is no other way. You must overcome your grief, or else you must pay the penalty.

The reason grief is so difficult to handle is that we are unable to change the cause. In metaphysics, we say "Change the cause, and you change the effect." The exception to this rule is grief. We cannot change the cause of sorrow, for we cannot restore him whose loss brought the sorrow on. What we must do is to change our reaction to our loss. If reaction determines the result, to change the reaction is to change the effect.

The thing most grief-stricken persons do not understand is that they are not dealing with the seeming tragedy that has befallen them, but with their thought about what has happened. It is your thought about death that makes you sad and not death itself. Underscore the words in the preceding sentence. Read them over many times. This understanding puts the responsibility of grief entirely up to the individual. When your sad thoughts and morbid memories have been erased, the pain of grief will lessen and finally disappear.

Death is not a unique phenomenon. It is not something that occurs only in your experience.

Everyone at some time in his life loses someone near and dear to him. Everyone dies at some time. Death is as natural and universal as birth and just as important. Grief will restore no one to life. Grief will bring no one comfort. Grief only saddens and distresses our friends. Those who refuse to be comforted in sorrow are, by their mobidity, bringing disease and discomfort to their bodies.

Why not face this matter squarely? Why not stop right now and ask yourself what you are really grieving about? Does a mother grieve over the graduation of a son or daughter? Does a man grieve over a promotion? Then why should we grieve over a spiritual coronation? If you did your utmost for the one who has gone from sight, if you did everything in your power to prolong his life, if you were kind, helpful, and considerate, there is nothing to grieve about.

It is easy during the period of intense grief to find causes for self-condemnation, for regret, for remorse. It is difficult to recall the constructive things one did, the patient steps one took, the impatient words which were held back. Part of the suffering in this area may have a basis in fact since our ideal usually outruns our performance, but much of it is likely to be fancied. We who are in the flesh can act only within the limits prescribed by our develop-ment and understanding. Your loved one, too, was in the flesh, and the responsibility for situations which now grieve you was, in all probability, mutual. There is no occasion for harrowing self-accusations.

Do you think that your loved one with his new-found understanding is condemning you? With his spiritual discernment, he now sees beneath the thought, beneath the act, beneath the result, and sees only the good. "Thou art of purer eyes than to behold evil and canst not look upon iniquity," said Habakkuk of God, whose attributes we share.

Try to consider the deceased from his point of view, not yours, and rejoice in his newly-attained freedom and his release from the weight of a worn-out or diseased body.

There is nothing terrible about slipping out of one body into another, about moving from one plane of consciousness to another. Man is spiritual, and his progress is ever upward.

Consider the new world of your loved one as com-pared to your own. Think what it means to be liv-ing in a state of peace that nothing can disturb.

Compare it with the suffering world in which you live. Be frank with yourself. Doesn't your grief tend to turn to envy? Perhaps that is why Jesus told us so little about the next phase of life. Knowing its joys in full would have created such dissatisfaction with this mortal phase that we wouldn't want to stay here. Doesn't that thought help you to consider the dead with joy instead of sorrow?

Why then do we meet the inevitable with such consternation? Why do we deck ourselves in black raiment and plunge ourselves into paroxysms of suffering? It would be more in keeping with our faith if we thanked God for the joy and happiness which those now gone from our sight once brought to us. You say that you believe in continuing life and a better world beyond. Why don't you act on your belief? Why don't you let nature take its course without rebelling? If no one died, there would be no room for oncoming generations. One generation dies that another may live. What must your loved ones think when they see your tear-dimmed eyes and hear your painful groans? Suppose someone kept you from going all the way with God. Suppose nature called you to make a complete departure from earth and you were held midway between the old and the new by the grief of some loved one.

Don't you see how difficult it must be for your loved one when you keep him earth-bound by your human love? Don't you owe something to the one who has started to make the change?

It is natural to grieve, and a certain amount of grief is a good thing. It becomes bad, however, when you keep it alive, that is, when you carry it beyond the normal period of mourning. To grieve over a loved one does not benefit him or you, and to capitulate to grief is weak and cowardly.

Most grief is selfish. We grieve for the same reason we publicize our aches and pains. We feel sorry for ourselves and want sympathy. That is the purpose of self-pity; it attracts the pity of others. Do you want that? Not at all. It is not pity that you want, but release. You don't want others to suffer because you suffer; you want to help relieve your suffering. That is why you turn to someone stronger and with greater understanding than yourself. The person who helps you most is not the person who sympathizes and commiserates with you, who sinks to your level of unhappiness, but the one who, having risen superior to grief, can show you the way out.

Self-pity is to grief what peritonitis is to an operation. It is poison. If your grief is free from self-pity, it will heal quickly. If it is fraught with self-pity, it will become infected and spread through your entire body. It is good for you to discuss your problem with your minister or a close friend because it is good to get your sorrow out into the open. It is bad, on the other hand, to broadcast your sorrows, that is, to tell them to everyone you meet.

The more you syndicate your problems, the more they grow. If you do not foster your grief, it will eventually die. You may not accept that statement today when the sun is dimmed, and the birds are still, and your heart is broken and crushed; but time is always on your side. When everything else fails, time heals. It is inconceivable that you could go on endlessly in your present state of mourning and misery. God has provided for your release by giving you the healing balm that comes with time. You will not forget the loved one who has gone from your sight, but you will achieve a closer and more intimate relationship with him.

Do you understand the principle we are trying to present in this study? Since time heals all wounds, and since we know that time is but a measurement of man's mind and that there is no time but NOW, the healing of your grief can take place just as easily while you are reading this page as it can in six months or a year. It all hinges on whether you accept the truth now or at some future time. If you accept facts now, you will escape the toll of a protracted and painful mourning.

Do you grieve because you think it is the proper way for you to show your respect and love for the departed? Then disabuse your mind of such a fallacious idea at once. The injury of such a grief is two-fold. It injures him, and it injures you. You must decide, therefore, whether you want to help your loved one or whether you want to hinder him. If you want to help him, you must heal your grief as quickly as possible; this is truly unselfish action.

THEY SHALL BE COMFORTED

Woven through God's own Word,
There is a silver thread:
"Blessed are they that mourn,
For they shall be comforted."
Never a promise fails
Out of the words He said.

Never one word has failed!
Cling to it, you who weep.
There will come hope again;
There will come peace and sleep.
Promises God has made
He will not fail to keep.

Lift up your weeping eyes;
Break of the daily bread.
God has taken, and God can keep
Safely your dear loved dead.
Walk with your hand in His;
You shall be comforted.

GRACE NOLL CROWELL

CHAPTER 3

This Is Eternal Life

"AND THIS IS LIFE ETERNAL THAT THEY MIGHT KNOW THEE, THE ONLY TRUE GOD . . ."

One of the greatest weaknesses of the old theology was its tense. We were always getting ready for something better. We were always preparing to meet God. We were always postponing our good until some future time. We were always looking forward to eternal Life.

In rational theology, we know that what shall be is NOW. *"Now is the accepted time"* for everything. *"Now is the day of salvation." "I am . . . the beginning and the end, saith the Lord." "God created man in his own image, in the image of God created he him." "Now are we the sons of God."* If God, Life, is the beginning and the end, and if we are created in His image, we too are eternal and are living in eternal life NOW. In fact, the only time we can ever live in eternal life is NOW.

Does that last sentence seem incredible to you? Work it out for yourself. Weigh the facts, and reach your own conclusion. If you are ever to have eternal life, you must have always had eternal life. Eternity stretches just as far in one direction as it does in the other. It stretches just as far backward as it does forward. But *backward* and *forward*, like *past* and *future*, are but measurements in time. If your departed loved one *was*, he *is*. That which shall be has always been and is NOW. The meeting of past and future is always in the present. Dr. Claude Bragdon says, "Power over time is power over the present moment, because that is a cross-section of eternity."

HERE and NOW, we are living the only life we shall ever have. It is eternal. HERE and NOW, we are in the Presence of God. All those whom we have called dead are as close to us as our last thought about them. HERE and NOW, we can pierce the mist of the unseen world and experience it. It is all around us; it is in the very air that we breathe. HERE and NOW, we can have the quality of life that never ends. We can live in it by recognizing it as a present possession. This is the message that Jesus brought and whose truth He proved. Either the life we are living right now is eternal, or there is no such thing. If life had a beginning, it has an end. If it is death-dealing, it cannot be life-giving. If it is corruptible, it cannot be incorruptible. If it is mortal, it cannot be immortal. Life cannot be two things at the same time. Life knows no opposites. Death is a denial of the Allness of God.

What do you suppose would happen to the minds and bodies of men if everyone realized that there is no death? If everyone realized that he is immortal now? We cannot vouch for others, but we can prove the truth for ourselves and live henceforth in the freedom that comes with the acceptance of the fact of continuous life, of present immortality.

When *"the glory of the Lord is risen upon thee* [that is, when you get this realization]," . . . *"Thy sun shall no more go down; . . . for the Lord shall be thine everlasting light, and the days of thy mourning shall be ended, "* according to Isaiah. The sun has always been to man illumination, light, warmth, and life. Metaphysically, man's sun is illumination of Truth, understanding of Principle, realization of Life.

Ernest Holmes says in *This Thing Called Life:* "The sun is always shining and when we withdraw ourselves from the shadows of our own unbelief, we shall find that the 'days of our mourning' will be ended. Mourning suggests that something has been lost. We are sad because we have lost a loved one; we have lost our health, our fortune or something else that we hold dear. Isaiah suggests that our days of mourning will cease when we view the universe as it really is.

" '*Wilt thou be made whole?*' asked the great teacher. Standing in the midst of the multitude, he proclaimed that the kingdom of God is at hand. Perhaps there is not so great a gulf between heaven and earth as we have believed. Are we taking time daily to permit the sunshine of truth to penetrate the dark chambers of our mind? '*Wilt thou be made whole?*' is a suggestion to open the windows of our mind, to lift up the gates of our consciousness, that the eternal flow of light may find entrance."

"*This is life eternal, that they might know thee, the only true God.*" If we read these words in the letter, we miss their real import. Jesus is calling us to a quality of life and consciousness that is eternal NOW. If we know God and enter into His Presence, we are in Heaven this very moment. If we do not know God, if we are unconscious of His Presence, we are in hell. Since life is a state of consciousness, we are always in one place or the other. We make our own Heaven, and we make our own hell. Life always finds us in the place that is like our thought, or prevailing state of mind. "*Where the tree falleth, there shall it be.*" As we die, so shall we live. As we live, so shall we die. Always we take our state of consciousness with us. We take it with us because it is our life. There is no after-life; but there is an unbroken continuation of this life. When we die, we go from where we left off here. That is why St. Paul urged Timothy to *"lay hold on eternal life"* while he was still living in the flesh.

There is no long sleep in a grave; there are no rewards or punishments. We but experience the things which are like our consciousness. If we take Heaven with us when we leave here, we shall find Heaven over there. If we take hell with us, we shall find it on the other side.

There are many rooms in the Father's House just as there are many grades in school. The period of time we spend on earth is but one grade of life. It is but a beginning. The Principle of Growth and Unfoldment is unlimited. That is why Jesus likened the Kingdom of Heaven to a grain of mustard seed.

Lewis L. Dunnington explains the continuity of Life in this way: "When He said to the thief on the cross, 'Today thou shalt be with me in Paradise,' He was not making an exception of the thief. He was saying that all men go right on living the moment the spirit body is released from the physical body at death. No long sleep in a grave—just a stepping over from one room in the Father's House to another."

Is this concept of eternity hard to understand? Then let us analyze it metaphysically. To get the inner meaning, we must leave our ordinary every-day consciousness and join Christ in His consciousness. We must differentiate between the human sense of time as measured by the clock and the calendar, and real time which embraces only the NOW. Everything that ever has been or ever will be is NOW. Where we are now is where we shall be through all eternity. Jay Cook tells us that "Life to the individual is just that instant of consciousness, at the instant of which his knowing faculty is aware." Now hold that idea for a moment while we analyze our own thinking about Heaven and eternal Life.

Where is Heaven and how are we going to reach it? The old theology represented Heaven as a future, far-off world to be reached only through death. But that concept of Heaven makes it unattainable. It presents two insurmountable barriers. One must not only accept Heaven as a future state but must also accept the belief that one is dead. Our present understanding of mental and spiritual Law is that in order to know anything, one must not only be alive but aware. Then how could one ever know that he was dead? He could know it only by being dead and alive at the same moment.

"This is life eternal that they might know Thee, the only true God." The only place which we can know God is within our own consciousness. We cannot enter Heaven through death, for we cannot be conscious and unconscious at the same time.

"Awake thou that sleepest, and arise from the dead, and Christ shall give thee light." If there is no death, why are we talking about what goes on after death? Perhaps we should remind ourselves that we are not dealing with death but with our thoughts about death. If death were real, there could be no resurrection. St. Paul placed the whole responsibility of death and resurrection squarely upon the shoulders of man. *"Since by man came death, so by man came also the resurrection of the dead."* How can man accomplish resurrection? By lifting up all the dead thoughts and dead conceptions which he has buried within himself and giving them their freedom in his thought. Since man conceived the erroneous idea of death, it is man who must reverse the lie in his own thought.

Are you grieving over a departed loved one whose body you have laid away? Are you thinking of him as dead? Then you should remind yourself that he is dead only in you and not in himself. You have shut him out of your life by a feeling of separation.

You have lost him because of your belief that he is dead, but he has not lost you. Jesus said, *"Let the dead bury their dead."* If you believe that you have buried your loved one, it is you who are dead and not he. You are dead in the sense that you have experienced the belief in death. Until you get beyond the limitations of flesh and blood, our earnest desire to assuage your grief can do little for you.

The whole thing, you see, goes on within your mind and not outside of it. If someone were dying or dead outside of your mind, you could not know anything about it. In sorrow, you think and speak of your loved one as having departed from his body, but the truth is that he was never in the body. Your loved one is Consciousness. He is a spiritual, not a physical being. His body, like yours, is but a mental concept.

J. Allen Boone says: "I do not do any dying myself. It has to be the other fellow, always the other fellow. Not me. I have to keep alive to do the thinking about it. No thinking about it on my part, then no dying by the other fellow on his part. Unless I am vitally there with my thinking to say so, there can be no dying or death anywhere. I am my own universe, my own mental universe. I can know and experience only what goes on in this universe. So that puts the whole question of death squarely up to me as an individual thinker. There can be no evasion, no quibbling. For me to be able to identify anyone or anything, the person or thing must be in my individual world of awareness, in my own mind or consciousness. Being in there, I am responsible for them, for I am the one who does the thinking about them.

"That places an enormous obligation on me, doesn't it? It means that if anyone dies he goes through the process within the areas of my own mind, or consciousness, over which I am supposed to rule supreme. I am the one that has to say that someone is dying for it to be a fact as far as I am concerned. I put the death sentence upon him. I pronounce him dead. I break the connection between us. I dig the grave and cover him up or cremate him. I rule that he has disappeared from my experience, probably forever. It all goes on within the borders of my own mind, or consciousness, with my consent, with my approval, with my help.

"A ghastly business, isn't it? Now it seems logical that if I should persist in such mentally destructive, mortuary practices, only one thing can happen. I shall transform this individual world of awareness of mine into a vast cemetery, filled with decaying, dying and dead concepts about a creation which God, in the beginning, is reported to have pronounced 'very good.' "

Do you see what we are trying to bring out in this chapter? We are trying to help you see the real self of your loved one. When you can do that, you will lose your sense of separation and loss. *"There is a natural body, and there is a spiritual body."* The natural body is visible, temporary, transient, and corruptible. The Spiritual body is invisible, eternal, and incorruptible. The first is limited; the second is unlimited, infinite, exhaustless.

According to Bishop Austin Pardue, "The physical or temporary body is used as an instrument by the real or spiritual body for the purpose of giving outward expression in a passing material world. It is to the spirit what a fountain pen is to the mind. Suppose that you have an idea you want to express via your pen. Should the pen break or become lost, does that mean that you no longer have a mind, feelings, love, character? Certainly, they are not lost just because you lost your fountain pen. If you lose your pen, you get a pencil, or a typewriter, or a dictaphone, or you communicate by word of mouth, or by prayer. The loss of a pen does not silence you forever any more than the loss of a physical body can stop you from living.

"In enjoying fellowship with the dead, or as the Prayer Book puts it, when 'we rejoice in their fellowship,' we must not think in terms of flesh and bones. You can never see the real me so long as you look at me with your physical eyes. You can see my hands, my feet, and my body, you can even see my eyes, through which I look out upon the physical world; but you cannot see the real me which is my soul, my character, my sins, my virtues, my hopes. Yet what am I but the sum total of the component parts of my spiritual body which is invisible and indestructible?"

"I am the resurrection, and the life: he that believeth in me, though he were dead yet shall he live; and whosoever liveth and believeth in me shall never die."

You do not have to die to be immortal; you are immortal now. The life you are now living is the only life you will ever have. It is birthless, deathless, eternal, and imperishable. You are an immortal being, and you exist in eternity NOW.

You are today in the midst of a life that has no end. If you accept this statement, you can no longer be afraid of death, for you know that there is no death for you. You have no fear of the future because you know that NOW is the only time there is, that the NOW is eternal—without beginning and without end. You become aware that you no longer need prepare for the future with the dread of death staring you in the face when you know that life must be lived in the present or not at all. In this consciousness, every day that you live takes you further away from death and the cemetery.

When you go along with God in the living Present, you realize that death is but an appearance. Because you are associating with God in the NOW, you no longer fearfully prepare to meet Him in some future time. You recognize Heaven all about you, and you let it become a part of you. You have a new security, for you realize that YOU ARE IMMORTAL NOW. Your fears are dissipated, for you know that anything you may need hereafter, God is providing NOW. *"Believest thou this?"* The whole faith of the Christian church rests upon this premise.

On one occasion when Jesus was addressing the Sadducees, He said, ". . . *As touching the resurrection of the dead, have ye not read that which was spoken unto you by God, saying, I am the God of Abraham, and the God of Isaac, and the God of Jacob?" "For he is not a God of the dead, but of the living; for all live unto Him. "* Do you get the impact of these words? He is saying that Abraham, Isaac, and Jacob are not asleep in a grave but are living now. Did not Jesus talk with Moses and Elijah on the Mount of Transfiguration after they had been dead hundreds of years? They were not asleep in a grave, nor is your loved one. Flesh and blood cannot inherit the Kingdom of Heaven because they have no place in the spiritual world. On this side of the veil, we have two bodies. On the other side of the veil, we shall have only one.

According to science, I have already had many bodies. I have only to turn to the family album to convince myself that this is true. The body of my infancy is not the body of my childhood. The body of my childhood is not the body of my youth; nor is the body of my youth that of my manhood. The body of my manhood will not be the body of my old age. Where have all these bodies gone? If I get a new body every seven years, where are the old bodies? I do not know, and it does not matter. The only thing that does matter is that I am still conscious of being the individual that I was in the first body I ever had. Every particle of my body has changed many times since I entered it, and yet it is the same body. My body is not me but mine. These various bodies belong only temporarily to me, but I continue to be one and the same individual despite the change in bodies.

Plato likened the human body to a river: "The water changes, but the river remains the same." What did Jesus mean when He said, *"I am the resurrection and the Life?"* He meant that identity is preserved though the material of the body be changed. The Principle of identity never perishes; it is never destroyed in all the changes and fluctuations of the material organism; it survives even the shock of death. Our conclusion must, therefore, be that although the natural (physical) body belonging to the material world is in a constant state of flux, spiritual man himself is birthless, deathless, and imperishable.

"As we have borne the image of the earthly, we shall also bear the image of the heavenly." The greatest sin is not to know that we are spirit — not to know that we are risen with Christ. The greatest error is to identify our loved ones with the body and death; to do so is to cut ourselves off from them. The message of the New Testament is that here and now we are immortal; that here and now we can enter into Eternal Life and let it become a part of us. Like every other spiritual quality and attribute, immortal life is a present possession. Would you survive what you call death? Then, the New Testament says, you must have in your consciousness an eternal quality; you must believe in a power within

you instead of a power over you; you must not seek the living among the dead. *"This is life eternal, that they might know Thee, the only true God, and Jesus Christ whom thou hast sent."* The New Testament calls you to a kind of thinking and living in which death has no part.

When Martha's brother lay dead, Jesus said to her, *"Whosoever liveth and believeth in Me* [that is, whoever harmonizes his mind with Mine and, sharing my quality of consciousness, recognizes that he is immortal now] *shall never die* [that is, death is powerless to touch him]."

"The hour is coming, and now is, when the dead shall hear the voice of the Son of God: and they that hear shall live." Death is but another side to life; until you know that and stop burying your dead within yourself, you will be dead indeed. You overcome death when you stop believing in it and postulate life. You must enter into it and live by it. You must stop referring to people as dying or dead. To say that they have passed over, or that they have made the change, is a more accurate statement.

"But some man will say, How are the dead raised up? and with what body do they come? Thou fool, that which thou sowest is not quickened, except it

die: . . . it is sown in corruption; it is raised in incorruption: it is sown in dishonour; it is raised in glory: it is sown in weakness; it is raised in power: it is sown a natural body; it is raised a spiritual body. . . . Now this I say, brethren, that flesh and blood cannot inherit the Kingdom of God; neither doth corruption inherit incorruption. Behold I shew you a mystery; We shall not all sleep, but we shall all be changed. In a moment, in the twinkling of an eye, at the last trump: for the trumpet shall sound, and the dead shall be raised incorruptible, and we shall be changed. For this corruptible must put on incorruption, and this mortal must put on immortality. . . . Therefore, my beloved brethren, be ye steadfast, unmovable, always abounding in the work of the Lord, forasmuch as ye know that your labour is not in vain in the Lord."

To receive the comfort inherent in this lesson, you must find that something within yourself that is always the same, something that is fixed and immovable. Jesus showed his awareness of the Indwelling God when he said, *"I AM the resurrection and the life."* To establish a sense of security and confidence, you must realize that there is no coming or going, for there is no separation in Spirit.

THERE IS NO DEATH

There is no death! Our stars go down
To rise upon some fairer shore;
And bright in heaven's jewelled crown,
They shine for evermore.

There is no death! The dust we tread
Shall change beneath the summer showers
To golden grain, or mellow fruit,
Or rainbow-tinted flowers.

The granite rocks in powder fall
And feed the hungry moss they bear;
The fairest leaves drink daily life
From out the viewless air.

There is no death! The leaves may fall;
The flowers may fade and pass away.
They only wait through wintry hours
The coming of the May.

And, ever near us, though unseen,
The fair immortal spirits tread;
For all the boundless universe
Is life. There are no dead!

JOHN L. MCCREERY

CHAPTER 4

The Dead Are the Living

*"BEHOLD, I AM ALIVE FOREVER
MORE."*

Those who sorrow are still asking the question
that Job asked more than three thousand years ago:
"If a man die, shall he live again?" You recall that
he answered the question himself when he added:
*"For there is hope of a tree, if it be cut down, that
it will sprout again, that the tender branch thereof
will not cease."*

"Is my loved one asleep in a grave awaiting some
future resurrection?" asks the sorrowing soul. "Is
there any means of communicating with him? Is
there any tangible proof of immortality?" If we can
answer these questions, the sting of death will have
been removed. No longer thinking of those who
have departed as asleep in a grave, we shall have the
same relation to them spiritually as we formerly had
physically. When we think of them, we shall think
of them in the same way that we think of a loved
one who has changed his place of residence, let us

say from New York to San Francisco. Although his body is out of sight, we do not challenge the fact of his existence.

We used to think of Eternal Life as a state of perfection to be reached through death. We now know that it is a present possession. *"This is Life eternal, to know Thee."* In other words, the life we are now living is the only life we shall ever have. It is not snipped off at one end, for it had no beginning. That is what Jesus meant when He said, *"Before Abraham was, I am."* Life is like a circle that is forever expanding or contracting. Man, made in the image and likeness of God, is co-existent with His Creator. *"Lord, Thou hast been our dwelling place in all generations."* Life did not begin when we were born; nor does it cease when we die. Life is eternal. Man lives, and moves, and has his being in God.

Where, then, do birth and death come in? Birth and death appear only on the relative or time plane. They are simply incidents in time.

Immanuel Kant wrote: "This world's life is only an appearance, a sensuous image of the pure, spiritual life and the whole world of sense; only a picture swimming before our present knowing faculty like a dream, and having no reality in itself.

For if we should see things and ourselves as they are, we should see ourselves in a world of spiritual natures, with which our entire real relation neither began at birth nor ends with the body's death."

Is that hard for you to accept? Then close your eyes and relax, and try to prove it to yourself. Try to think of yourself in the pre-birth state before you were conceived. You can't think of yourself as nonexistent, can you? Why not? Because you are consciously thinking. What does this prove? It proves that *you were* before you were born. Now do the same thing with death. Try to imagine yourself as having died and attending your own funeral service. You can't do that, can you? Why not? Because you are thinking of yourself as consciously being there. What does this prove? That you did not die at all. You did not die because you cannot be conscious and unconscious, present and absent, at the same time.

What is the human belief about death? It is a belief in unconsciousness, is it not? Then for a man to experience death in his consciousness (which is his life), he would have to be conscious and unconscious at the same time. In other words, he would have to know that he was dead, and if he knew anything at all, he would know that he was not dead.

Where, then, do the so-called dead go? They don't go anywhere. Heaven is all around us, and we are just as much in it now as we ever shall be. There is no "Beautiful Isle of Somewhere," and there is no future for you, or for your loved ones, or for anyone else. There is only *here-and-now,* and the *here-and-now* is eternal. Life and death are not two worlds but two aspects of one world. I repeat that there are no dead. There are only people in two states of consciousness. They live on two planes, and God rules both.

Jay Cook analyzes the nature of consciousness in this way: "Can you live in any thing except that which to you is present? Suppose you admit that Heaven is a far-off, future plane to be reached after you had accepted the belief that you were dead, when would you reach it? You could not reach it until you knew that you were dead, and if you knew anything you would know that you were not dead.

"So if you admit the possibility of a future state it becomes eternally a future state in relation to you. Knowledge is always related to the knower, and you exist as a knower of that knowledge; and there is nothing but here and now to that knower. Thus if you admit the possibility of a future state, you can never catch up with it this side of eternity and cannot live in it at all. How would you know you were living in it? If you did live in it you would have to live in it as a present state."

St. Paul said, *"For since by man came death, by man came also the resurrection of the dead."* Notice the words *by man.* This statement places the sole responsibility for death and for resurrection squarely upon the shoulders of man. If death is a man-made belief, as St. Paul says, only man can overcome it. He can overcome it by the recognition of himself and others as spiritual beings living in a spiritual world now. This truth excludes the material man who was supposed to die. *"Henceforth know we no man after the flesh,"* said St. Paul. *"Call no man your Father upon the earth,"* admonished Jesus. *"Know ye not that your body is the temple of the Holy Ghost which is in you?"* What is the Holy Spirit in man? It is that something within him that was never born, never gets sick, and never dies. Until we know this truth, we shall continue to experience "burying the dead."

In *There Is Nothing But God,* Vivian May Williams says that "Since no one can actually experience death in his own consciousness, he can only appear to be dead to the other fellow; hence Jesus' remark, 'Let the dead [deluded in consciousness] bury their dead.' The ones who believe that they bury their loved ones are the 'dead' ones, for they experience the belief in death. In order to experience a thing, you must be conscious of it. Since the belief in death is unconsciousness, it would be necessary for one to function in unconsciousness while still in a state of consciousness, in order for him to die. As this is an utter impossibility, there is but one conclusion—that death is pure delusion, and can be transcended by anyone who catches the vision of his own Eternal Life, which is his own omnipresent consciousness. While they were still on earth, Jesus and John proved this great truth, that Heaven is a state of mind, rather than a locality to be reached by experiencing such a negative belief as death. When each and every individual strives to overcome the belief in death in his own mind, then the last enemy will be destroyed as readily as we heal disease and then we will all awaken in consciousness to the eternal facts of life. It is logical to presume that those from whom we appear to have been separated by the false concept of death have never changed, for Life is changeless. The constant belief in death, which includes separation and grief, distorts the vision and prevents one from seeing reality—hence individuals are unseen by those who believe 'they bury their dead.' Believing in death can affect one's business and supply as well as the body, for it is a belief in the cessation of life which is all activity. When one ceases to believe in death, he will have less disease, for fear of death induces physical discomfort. Fear of disease induces poverty, for if one does not have money for food, he believes he must die. People are afraid of the elements, for they believe in death and destruction. Individuals are afraid to travel for fear of accidents and death. In fact, every limitation can be traced to the 'last enemy,' death. All one needs to do is to reason logically from the basis of absolute truth in order to clear his consciousness of the false belief which causes more apparent grief than any other. First of all, we are spiritual beings—this fact excludes a 'material' man who is supposed to die. Heaven is here around us; so we cannot go to any other place."

Eternal Life is a quality of consciousness to be experienced now. It depends not upon length but upon death. When we live deeply, we are not concerned about the body, time, or anything else. Eternal Life is our own, here and now. Some day we shall leave the body in which we live, but that will not trouble us. Since *"God is Life,"* as Jesus said, and since our life is His Life, for we are made in His image and likeness, how can we die? Can God die? Can a part of God's image be lost? Can that which had no beginning have an end? Is the body the man, or is it an instrument which he uses?

John Quincy Adams was met by a contemporary on the streets of Boston on his eightieth birthday, and was asked, "How is my friend John Quincy Adams?" He answered in words that have since become classic: "John Quincy Adams himself is very well, thank you, but the house he lives in is sadly dilapidated. It is tottering on its foundations. The walls are badly shattered, and the roof is worn. The building trembles in every wind, and I think John Quincy Adams will have to move before long. But he himself is very well."

"Thou fool," says St. Paul, *". . . thou sowest not that body that shall be."* Someone has developed the analogy in these words: "Anyone who has sown a seed and watched it grow knows that the tender plant which comes up is not the brown seed which was sown. The seed, as we know it, dies and mingles with the earth, but from within rises the green, vivid shoot which has the power to move mountains.

"Thus it is with the physical body: when it is no longer a fit instrument for the soul, it dies and returns to the elements from which it came; but from within, the Spiritual Being, the Real Man, rises, not out of the tomb, but from around the body. The Soul, the Real Man, keeps the same essential identity and the same spiritual individuality; only the outer cover, the integral atoms are changed."

Here is another uncredited but pertinent comparison: "The beautiful phenomenon of the rainbow is a partial analogy of the principle of identity made manifest by atoms that are in a perpetual flux. Stretching across the sky in its majesty of blending, prismatic colors, the rainbow appears to be fixed, substantial, solid; but every particle of it is changing thousands of times as one gazes at the arch of color. It is composed of shifting, whirling atoms, but the atoms are the vehicles, the manifestations without which you could not see the analysis of the beam of light.

"When the falling rain drops cease, the rainbow is gone, but the BEAM OF LIGHT is still shining as brightly as before. When a man 'dies,' we cannot see him, because the combination of atoms in flux which composed the vehicle of his manifestation has passed into new combinations. However, his glowing identity is as truly in existence as is the beam of light that formed the rainbow."

What we speak of as life beyond the grave is simply that part of life which we do not see. That there is such a life is well authenticated by the factual demonstrations of those who have returned to prove it. Jesus said, *"I go to prepare a place for you."* He did not describe or locate this place in time except to say that it is within and around man and is everywhere equally present. *"For we know that if our earthly house of this tabernacle were dissolved, we have a building of God, an house not made with hands, eternal in the heavens."*

If we accept God as THE WHOLE, we cannot continue to accept two kinds of men—one dead and the other alive. Why not? Because *"God is not the God of the dead, but of the living: for all live unto Him."* Do you see now why it is so necessary for you to make your agreement with death?

Alexander Maclaren has given us the memorable words, *"THE DEAD ARE THE LIVING,"* in the paragraph that follows: "Every man that has died is at this instant in full possession of all his faculties, in the intensest exercise of all his capacities, standing somewhere in God's Universe, ringed by a sense of God's Presence, and feeling in every fibre of his being that life, which comes after death, is not less real, but more real, is not less great, but more great, not less full or intense, but more full and intense, than the mingled life, which, lived here on earth, was a center of life surrounded with a crust and circumference of immortality. THE DEAD ARE THE LIVING. They lived while they died; and after they die, they live on forever."

The ancients had less difficulty in accepting spiritual evidences than we who live in this complex modern world and who are not wholly aware that the old adage, "A little learning is a dangerous thing," is true. The Scriptures contain many records of incidents pertinent to our acceptance of belief in life after death.

One of the strongest of these is reported in three of the Gospels. They state that, according to the personal testimony of Peter, James, and John, Jesus was transfigured (Luke says *"The fashion of his countenance was altered"* and Mark reports *"His raiment became shining, exceeding white as snow; so as no fuller on earth can white them"*) and after the Transfiguration, talked with Moses and Elias. Now Moses had been dead for fifteen hundred years, and it had been about nine hundred years since the translation of Elijah. Only one Gospel attempts to give the purport of their conversation, but each treats it as a natural event which arouses no particular excitement or wonder.

The touching story of the little lad who died of sun stroke, when he, as small lads are wont to do, went out to the field where his father was reaping, is dear to the hearts of all parents. All mothers and fathers recognize the situation, for when the child cried to his father, *"My head! My head!,"* the father told another lad to *"Carry him to his mother."* She, you will recall, held him *"on her knees till noon and then he died."* In that humble home, a room had been prepared for Elisha who passed by continually as he went to and from his labors. The much-wanted child came as a reward for the thoughtfulness of the *"great woman"* when the couple had long despaired of having children. What more natural then that the Shunammite woman should lay her child on the bed of the man of God, and go for him herself?

When Elisha saw her from afar off, he sent his servant to learn why she had come, directing him to ask, *"Is it well with thee? Is it well with thy husband? Is it well with the child?"* Despite her answer, *"It is well,"* she kept on till she met Elisha. He, recognizing the emergency, sent his servant to lay his staff upon the child, but there was *"neither voice, nor hearing"* in him.

"And when Elisha was come unto the house, behold, the child was dead, and laid upon his bed. He

went in therefore, and shut the door upon them twain, and prayed unto the Lord. And he went up, and lay upon the child, and put his mouth upon his mouth, and his eyes upon his eyes, and his hands upon his hands: and he stretched himself upon the child; and the flesh of the child waxed warm. Then he returned, and walked in the house to and fro; and went up, and stretched himself upon him: and the child sneezed seven times, and the child opened his eyes."

In the thirteenth chapter of the book of II Kings, we read that during this time of great wickedness and strife, a funeral procession set upon by an invading band cast the dead man into the sepulchre of Elisha. *"And when the man was let down, and touched the bones of Elisha, he revived and stood upon his feet."*

We have, too, the story of the restoration by Jesus of another child, the twelve-year-old daughter of Jairus, one of the rulers of the synagogue. Jairus *besought Him greatly saying, "My little daughter lieth at the point of death: I pray thee, come and lay thy hands upon her that she may be healed; and she shall live."* Jesus was delayed in his journey to the home by the people who *"thronged Him"* and by the interruption of the woman of great faith who touched *"but His clothes."* Just at this moment, a messenger came to Jairus with the words, *"Thy daughter is dead; trouble not the Master!"* Jesus, undeterred by the news, pursued his way with confidence, saying, *"Fear not, believe only, and she shall be made whole."* At the home, he told those who wept, *"She is not dead, but sleepeth."* Did they believe Him? No. *"They laughed Him to scorn, for they knew that the girl was dead."* What did Jesus do then? He cleared the room of all but the parents, and Peter, James, and John; then taking the girl by the hand, He commanded, *"Maid, arise."* *"Her spirit came again and she arose straightway."* Now note the words, *"and her spirit came again."* Where had it been? From whence did it come? Certainly not from death nor from annihilation.

Perhaps you recall the case of the only son of the widow of Nain whose grief at the death of her son was shared by *"much people of the city."* The dismal funeral procession was making its way out of the city to the burying ground when they met Jesus and a small band of His followers going into the city. The air was rent with the cries and sobs of the mourners when Jesus, touched by their sorrow, reached out His hand, and restored the lad to life again with the words, *"Young man, I say unto thee,*

Arise." The account goes on: *"And he that was dead sat up and began to speak."*

St. John tells us that Lazarus, the brother of Mary and Martha, had lain in the grave for four days before Jesus came to Bethany. Decomposition, of course, had already begun in his body, but Jesus said, *". . . if thou wouldst believe, thou shouldst see the glory of God."* Then after thanking God for hearing Him, He called with a loud voice, *"Lazarus, come forth. And he that was dead came forth."* There were many witnesses to this miracle; perhaps the most credible ones were the enemies of Lazarus who vowed then and there to put him to death again. There could not have been any doubt about his resurrection nor the lesson which Jesus intended to convey—that *there are no dead.* If Lazarus had not been alive in some other sphere of activity, he could not have occupied his body a second time.

There are other proofs of resurrection and of life beyond the grave, such as those recorded of Tabitha and Eutychus, but the greatest of these was given by Jesus himself. Thirty thousand young Jewish men of military age were crucified around the walls of Jerusalem by Titus and Pontius Pilate; the name of only one of these is known to us today.

Why? Because only one returned to this earth and took up his Life and ministry again.

And what are we to deduce from these irrefutable demonstrations? What lesson is there in them for us? *"The dead are the living."* If the dead come back, they must have been alive on some other plane. The belief in death is the only death there is. Jesus said to the dying thief on the cross: *"Today shalt thou be with me in Paradise."* Not ten thousand years from now. Not on the judgment day, but *now.* There is "no long sleep in a grave; just a stepping over from one room in the Father's House to another."

GOD OF THE LIVING

God of the living, in whose eyes
Unveiled thy whole creation lies,
All souls are thine; we must not say
That those are dead who pass away,
From this our world of flesh set free;
We know them living unto thee.

Released from earthly toil and strife,
With Thee is hidden still their life;
Thine are their thoughts, their works, their
    powers:
All thine, and yet most truly ours;
For well we know, where'er they be,
Our dead are living unto Thee.

Thy word is true, thy will is just.
To Thee we leave them, Lord, in trust,
And bless Thee for the love which gave
Thy Son to fill a human grave
That none might fear that world to see
Where all are living unto Thee.

JOHN ELLERTON

CHAPTER 5

The Friendly Enemy

In some unexplained way, word got around that a certain friend of mine had died. When he heard the rumor, he said, "In the language of Mark Twain, I must say that 'the report of my death is greatly exaggerated' — and at the same time, I must admit there is truth in the report."

Could his statement be true? Can a man be dead and alive at the same time? Yes, in the way that St. Paul died daily. My friend was not talking about the total death of his body but about partial death. Partial death is putting off the old and putting on the new; it is, in a sense, being dead and alive at the same time. Partial death is a continuous process, but to die daily is to be born daily.

Robert Collier says: "Older cells slow down, break away and are thrown out. This is how a dog follows the scent of his master — by the trail of the old discarded cells that he is continually throwing off. It is only when we fail to throw off the inharmonious cells that disease gets a foothold and we sicken or die."

Why, then, do we think of death as an enemy instead of a beneficent power opening the gates of immortality unto us? Because we believe that the body is the self of us. Because we believe that life depends upon bones, brain, muscle, skin, and tissue. Because we are judging according to appearances.

The materialist says, "Death is a calamity. Death is a destroyer. Death is oblivion. Death is desolation. Death is eternal darkness. Death is a frightful abyss. Death is the final summons." But according to St. Paul, the only death to be fearerd is *"to be carnally minded."* What does that mean? Who are the carnally minded? They are those who give no thought to God or to spiritual things in this life. Living by temporary, transient, and fugitive values, they abide in darkness. Having nothing eternal in their natures, there is nothing for them to hold to when they are faced with the evidence of the temporary quality of the physical body. Believing that life had a beginning, they believe that it must also have an end.

Now answer this question: "Is your body you or is it yours?"

J. Allen Boone answers the question in this way: "Your body is yours. But not you. It is no more you — that is, the *real* you — than your overcoat, or your automobile, or your fountain pen. YOU ARE

CONSCIOUSNESS. You are a mental, not a physical, being. That which you have been calling your body is a mental concept. It may appear to be physical substance. It may seem to be and feel very real. But sooner or later you will be compelled, in one way or another, to realize that it is a mental concept, a formation of your own thinking, and so subject to your own thinking."

Let us think for a moment about total death, or the simultaneous death of all parts of the body. When a man is said to be dead, what is it that has died? What is it that alone feels the power of death? The body. What is the body? A temporary habitation, or covering for the spirit. Why, then, did St. Paul say, *"For me to die is gain"?* Because perfect health depends upon a perfect balance between life and death. Life works from the top down; death works from the bottom up. The faster we die, the more alive we are. Consequently, death is not a stranger as so many think, for it is with us constantly. We die twenty-four hours a day; the process of death is at work in our bodies now. With every breath that we take and with every movement that we make, part of us dies.

Don't you see what a beneficent and salutary thing continual death is? We die momently in order that we may have more life. We die that we may be made new, strong, and vigorous for our daily tasks. We are dying all the time. Science tells us that we die completely every seven years. That is, we do not have one cell in our bodies today that we had seven years ago. We are constantly renewed by the process of partial death.

Then what is the difference between this continual or partial death and the final summons which the materialist calls the end? Merely this: one is gradual; the other is more abrupt. Does this mean that there are two processes of death? No, there is only one. Each is a gateway to more life, and each works in the body only. Then what happens to the soul through all these bodily changes? It lives on.

Man changes his clothes (body), but the essential self remains unchanged. If he has lived his three-score-and-ten years, he has already had ten bodies and ten sets of brains; yet he is still conscious of being the same individual that he was in the first body he ever had. He will continue to live on without a break and with scarcely a deflection. If the identity persists through the coming and going of ten bodies, surely it will persist forever.

Are you still puzzled over the materialistic conceptions of life with which St. Paul was so wrathfully intolerant? Then compare the statements in the second paragraph of this chapter with that thrilling fifteenth chapter of I Corinthians which in no uncertain terms proclaims that *"this corruptible must put on incorruption, and this mortal must put on immortality."* Compare them with the words of Jesus: *"I go to prepare a place for you." "God is not the God of the dead, but of the living; for all live unto Him." "Because I live, ye shall live also." "Whosoever liveth and believeth in me shall never die."*

Can it be that even His disciples had doubts? You recall that after he had stated, *"In my Father's house are many mansions,"* He said, *"If it were not so, I would have told you."* Do you get the import of these statements? If the Principle of that which lives in you is Life, it cannot know death, for death is a denial of the Principle of Life.

If we approach the subject from the natural side as St. Paul did, we shall see that birth and death are but two ends of the same thing—death to the old body and birth to the new. Death does not come to destroy us, but to help us into our new life. It is an escape, so to speak, from bodies which we have not yet learned how to redeem. The going-out is but a coming-in to victory and liberation, not to defeat and annihilation. St. Peter promised that *"an entrance shall be ministered unto you abundantly into the everlasting kingdom of our Lord and Saviour Jesus Christ.*" Alexander Maclaren says: "The going out is a coming in; the journey has two ends, only the two ends are so very near each other that the same act is described by the two terms. Looked at from this side, it is a going-out; looked at from the other side, it is a coming-in."

St. Paul listed death among our assets. Death in our present state of consciousness is just as important and necessary as birth. One of our lessons is to learn to think of it as a blessing. We must see the reality so that we may thank God for such a beneficent provision.

When we understand life, the sting of death is removed. Jesus was never startled nor upset by the announcement that someone had died; He broke up every funeral that He ever attended. He proved that there is no reason why we should grieve over death. If we had the proper perspective, perhaps we should grieve for the living and not for the dead.

In the truest sense, death is a purifying process. It opens a place to us in which former conditions and things have no power. Instead of fighting, struggling, praying, and working against adverse conditions, old age, physical and mental infirmities, and unsolved problems, man dies completely to them. All human limitations are centered in the cranial personality (fleshly mind) and continue as long as the cranial personality lasts. In this sense, death is the letting-go of the old pattern, of the manifestation on the physical plane; it is the taking-up of a new pattern without any leftovers, or recollections. *"The former things shall pass away; they shall not be remembered nor come into mind any more."* In other words, the so-called dead man comes under another set of beliefs altogether. The imperfect dies; the perfect lives on.

Elwood Worcester in *Making Life Better* brings this idea out beautifully. He says: "As long as the old brain exists, we must remain the old man. When it suffers, we suffer even to the point of losing our intelligence. In old age, it is worn out. Then it is time for us to leave it, just as once before we left a home no longer suitable for our habitation. More than one materialist has compared the brain to a harp, and consciousness and memory to the music flowing from its strings. When the harp is shattered by the hand of death, they say that is the end of the music. But does this figure hold? The tone of the harp sounds upon the air, and you hear it. The harp is shattered; for a moment you hear the music, then you hear it no more. But someone standing a little farther away still hears it. Then he, too, hears it no longer. Has the strain then ceased to vibrate? Not at all. It has only passed beyond the sphere of your quarter-of-an-inch-ear. Were your ear as large as the space those vibrations now occupy, or were you able to follow them as they go through the air, and not through the air only but through water, through stone walls, through thick and thin, you would still hear them singing on their way to the stars.

"When the brain is injured in this world, we suffer. But if the injury is so great that this life ends, that is the end of the injury. It can hardly follow us into the next life, since the greatest injury to the old life, which is death, is the very thing which makes the new life possible. This is a consolation to those who have insane or weak-minded friends. True dementia is a disease of the brain, and it will cease when the brain ceases. You imagine that because the mind shares the weakness of old age, it is a sign that it is about to cease to exist. But you might as well infer that because the mounting pendulum moves slowly and heavily and almost stands still when it reaches the limit of its oscillation, it is about to stop. On the contrary, it is just preparing to take a new stroke."

I am reluctant to introduce a thought in this book that might add to anyone's grief, but the acceptance of the thought presented up to this point results irrefutably in the acceptance of this fact: Since death works no great transformation in us, those who have given no serious thought to spiritual things in this life will find no immediate happiness or satisfaction in a realm where Spirit is the only reality.

Did you ever find yourself in a gathering of people where you were not expected or wanted? Do you remember how unhappy you were, how you wished that you hadn't come, and how you wondered how soon you could get away? Magnify that embarrassment a thousand times, and you will see something of the feelings and the predicament of the man who enters the next life as a stranger.

Don't you see why Heaven must begin here? It is because a shroud has no pockets. The only things that you can take with you from this life are the things that you have in your consciousness; that is, your thoughts, your feelings, and your will. Everything else must be left behind. To live in a spiritual environment over there, you must cultivate the consciousness of Spirit over here. That is what St. Paul meant when he said to Timothy, *"Lay hold on eternal life.*" The emphasis was upon the present moment. It is what Jesus meant when He said, *"This is life eternal that they might know thee, the only true God, and Jesus Christ whom thou has sent.*" Hold that for a moment while you consider the next great truth. If eternal life is dependent upon a knowledge of God, as Jesus said, and knowledge is always related to the knower, the Consciousness of Spirit must begin on earth. Why? Because a man always finds himself in that place or condition which is like his consciousness. If he finds Heaven here, he will find it there. If he doesn't find it here, he will have to wait for it over there. That is, he will have to wait until he cultivates a Consciousness of Heaven, or until he can function as a spiritual being.

That is why St. Paul said, *"To be carnally minded is death.*" The carnally-minded are the un-related or the blind of the spiritual world. Having seen nothing spiritual here, they will, for the time being, see nothing spiritual there. But *"The hour is coming, and now is, when the dead* [those without a knowledge of spiritual things] *shall hear the voice of the Son of God: and they that hear shall live.*"

But there is another group that must be considered in a book of this kind. When we speak of "the happy dead," we mean those who have died a natural death. When we speak of the unhappy dead, we mean those who have died an unnatural death.

The continuation of this life is pictured in the New Testament as a beautiful home — a prepared place. *"I go to prepare a place for you,"* said Jesus. For those who know and love God, death is very much like birth; it is a going-home. Just as a child at birth comes to a home in which preparations have been made for his arrival, so those who enter the higher life or Spirit are awaited by loved ones who have anticipated and eagerly desired their coming. Suicides, however, go before they are expected or wanted. A suicide is like the young man who goes to college and quits before he has finished his course, like the runner who leaves the race, the swimmer who stops in midstream. It is logical to assume that suicides in the next life are for a time, at least, the most miserable and unhappy of all those present.

Countless persons have given testimony at the time of their death as to the presence of those from whom they have been long separated. While there are many recorded instances, those most convincing to us occur within our own circle of friends and relatives. Most of us have known personally of cases in which persons at the moment of their passing have joyfully greeted loved ones who had earlier made the change.

The general belief of most people who give no thought to spiritual things is that the next life will somehow take care of itself. That cannot be true, for the next life is but a continuation of this life. We reap what we have sown, here or hereafter. The character of one is determined by the character of the other. Immortality is a quality of life that is begun here and carried with us across the line between the worlds in the experience we call death. It is a kind of thinking and living with which death has nothing to do.

"Eternal life is not a gift to be bestowed on the child of God hereafter; he hath eternal life. Immortality is not a bequest to be by and by received; it is a present possession," says Lyman Abbott. ". . . If I would have a right to the tree of life, if I would have the right to know that there is a tree of life, I must seek this immortal life here, and seek it from God who is here, and seek it through the channels He opens for us. . . . If we would have a rational hope in life hereafter, we must have immortal life here."

Whittier, too, expressed this thought:

> The tissue of the life to be
> We weave with colors all our own;
> And in the field of destiny
> We reap as we have sown.

Death, as we have seen, is not only necessary, but it is friendly. Perhaps you have never thought of the friendliness of death before. Death has many offices, and they are all good. To a man enjoying perfect health and prosperity or to the one who feels that the responsibility for the future of his family rests upon his shoulders alone, death may seem to be an enemy. We use the word *seem* because he is looking at only one segment of the picture. To the helpless and incurable invalid, death comes as a blessing.

Did you ever consider what a plight we should be in if there were no such thing as death? Suppose, for an instant, that we had to perpetuate these bodies in their present state through all eternity. Think of those who suffer from painful and incurable diseases. Would you have them go on in their agony forever? Can you imagine anything worse than living in the present body and the present world through eternity? Do you begin to see why death is a friend instead of an enemy? Death translates us out of darkness into light, out of captivity into freedom. No wonder that the body struggles to keep the spirit within its boundaries. When the self has gone, the body falls apart.

To quote Lyman Abbott again: "To be free from the perpetual decay of this earthly tabernacle, to be released from its pains and infirmities, to be emancipated from its clogs and incumbrances, to have the chrysalis break and to have the winged soul let loose — this hour of freedom is not to be dreaded before it comes, nor mourned afterward; but to be rejoiced in. Self sits by the tenantless prison cell and mourns; but love looks up and is glad that the prisoner has escaped into the liberty of the sons of God."

Do you face death with bitterness, desolation, terror, and excoriation? Then remember these truths. Death is not a malignant and vindictive power driving us toward a bottomless abyss. Death is but the limit of our horizon. There is more beyond. The best is yet to be. Death is a friend.

THEY CALLED HIM DEATH

They called him Death who sat beside me here,
His tender smile alight with comfortings—
They cried aloud in agony of fear,
    Hearing his wings.

He came with silver fingers, cool and kind,
To ease the pain of tortured, struggling breath.
With him were all the dreams I tried to find;
    They called him Death.

He bore me up in great strong arms of light.
Upon his lips a song that did not cease;
As like a shaft of flame, we cleft the night—
    I called him Peace.

VIRGINIA FOLEY

CHAPTER 6

The Second Coming

Many years ago, a sermon delivered by the Reverend John Maillard, of Milton Abbey, England, appeared in print. I present it here to you, hoping that you will find in it, as I did, a renewed confidence in the continuity of life.

"In one of the darkest moments of human history, Jesus said to His disciples in the upper room, *'I go away and come again unto you.'* We speak of our loved ones as having gone forth to that bourne from which no traveler returns; we say that we shall go to them but that they can not return to us. I want you to understand in the hallowed light of the Upper Room that this word of Jesus was a true word, true concerning Himself, and true of all those who are in his spiritual fellowship and consciousness and whose life is hidden with Him, in God.

" *'The gift of God,'* said St. Paul, *'is Eternal Life.'* Life was given once and for all; and though it appears to go through death, it is not dead. It is everlasting to every created thing. Nothing can take it away for a longer period than those fleeting seconds of transmission from one body to another when transient life ends and spiritual life begins. Death truly has no sting, and it is rapidly followed by a glorious victory which is given by God the Father, Son, and Holy Ghost. *'Believest thou this?'* It takes the deepest and finest powers to believe what Jesus believed, to feel the full force and meaning of what He said in the Upper Room under the shadow of death. As the representative of humanity, he said, *'I go away, and come again unto you.'*

"We all admit, of course, that our friends who are lost to our view come back to our thought and affection. They are lost to the eye and the ear, but not to the memory and to the heart. Indeed, there is a going-away which is a condition of coming-again with added power and glory. We lose a visible person; we gain an invisible life. We speak of painful separations; yet they are only the conditions of spiritual meeting. Out of the silence and darkness they come back to us—those whom we loved and thought we had lost—and their pure noble spirits, which flesh and blood had often hidden from us, come and take possession of our hearts and abide with us until the end of our days.

"How true that was in the case of Jesus and His Disciples! They were never farther from their

Master, those men of Galilee, than when they walked by His side. It was only when He was no more seen by them in the flesh, that He came to them as never before, that the finer Truth of His Being and Life shone in clear beauty upon them, that those matchless words of His were understood in their true meaning and were burned into their hearts like fire, that their eyes were opened and they knew Him.

"*'I go away and come again unto you.'* I repeat that these words are most truly fulfilled in every bereavement. For three dark days, our loved ones seem to lie in the grave. Then they come again — not to the house of the senses, but to the house of the soul — and we know them as never before, and love them as never before, and possess them as never before. This is not the language of fancy, but the fact. We have lost their visible presence, but we have gained their invisible companionship, a presence to be felt and known in darkness and in light forever. Although this is much, it is not all. It is not only to thoughts, to memory, and to imagination that these happy dead return — they come also mind to mind, soul to soul, spirit to spirit. The Communion of Saints is something other and higher than communion. I am, of course, not talking of what is known as spiritualism. No, not that—and yet, somehow we know that the ones we love do come back, though we see nothing and hear nothing.

"'Lo, I am with you always.' We repeat that there is no hereafter for the ones who are in God. THERE IS ONLY HERE. There is no future, far-off world for our loved ones or for us. That world of perfection is all about us—in the air we breathe, in the world in which we live and move, in every realm which we may explore. It is not the barriers of time and space which separate us from it—it is our slavery to our senses, our worldliness, our self-ishness, our sin. It was Jesus who taught that the worlds are not far apart. He lived Himself in close and constant communion with both, and He meant for His followers and disciples to live as He lived.

"The early Church, drawing its inspiration from Christ, realized that, whether in the body or out of it, her members were still united in the same Holy Communion of worship and of service. They dwelt, not so much on future reunion, as on present fel-lowship, and all through the ages there have been those among the sanest, wisest, and best of men to whom the spiritual influence of the dead—that is, of the living who have passed within the veil—has been a present and precious reality.

"I go away and come again unto you!" Does the program stop when you turn off the radio in your home? Aren't the invisible voices, newscasts, and orchestras still playing in your home even though you do not hear them? Does turning off your receiving set affect the program? Then what have you disconnected, the program or the physical instrument called the radio? Does turning off your radio make any difference, as far as the continuance of the program is concerned? The radio is but a symbol of the omnipresence and continuity of life, and it helps us to understand why death does not end life, why it does not stop the functioning of the individual. Man is not a body, but a soul. He does not have a soul. He IS a soul. The soul simply uses the body as a vehicle of expression. Thus death is but a process of dropping one means of expression for another. It does not mean that life has stopped, but that man expresses and functions in more life than ever before. Whereas, before, he functioned on three planes, now he functions on four planes. He now lives in the City Four-square, where there is no night — nor darkness of death, nor sorrow, nor grief, nor human thinking. Our communication must now be spiritual, instead of physical.

The following apt and comforting paragraph comes from an unknown source:

"I am standing upon a busy wharf. A ship at my side spreads her white sails to the morning breeze and starts out upon the ocean. She is an object of beauty and strength, and I stand there watching her until, at length, she hangs like a speck of white cloud just where the blue sea and blue sky mingle with each other as one. Then, someone at my side says, 'There! She is gone.' Gone where? Gone from my sight, that is all. She is just as large in mast and hull and spar as she was when she left my side, and just as able to bear her load of living freight to the place of her destination. Her diminished size is in me, not in her. And just at the moment when some-one at my side is saying, 'There! She's gone,' there are other eyes watching her coming, and other souls take up the glad shout, 'Here she comes!' And that is dying."

"Life is eternal; love is immortal; and death is only a horizon; and a horizon is nothing save the limit of our sight," says Raymond Rossiter in his Commendatory Prayer.

Since poetry is the natural language of the emotions, and since we all find it difficult to separate our thoughts about death from our feeling about it, there are many beautiful poems on the subject. The author of the poem that follows is unknown.

In all this glory, shall I have no part?
  Upon life's tapestry spin no design?
Must I, like some stray wind, depart,
  And, on the earth, leave no remembered
    sign?

Surely I have not lived to court decay
  And mingle with the cold insensate earth!
Why, even flowers, after their brief stay,
  Come back again. Each spring sees their
    rebirth!

And I am less than flower, less than tree,
  Which dying, birth again? The ages hold
Inviolate the secret; but to me
  Still clings the thought: I am diviner
    mold.

If you should miss me on some quiet morn,
  Grieve not! We only die to be reborn.

CHAPTER 7

Where Are the Dead?

Where are the dead? Before we can answer the question, we must understand our relationship to Life. We must realize that we are spiritual beings with fourth-dimensional powers functioning on the three-dimensional earth but transcending it.

Wordsworth sensed this fact as he wrote the "Ode on Intimations of Immortality."

> Our birth is but a sleep and a forgetting;
> The soul that rises with us, our life's Star,
> Hath had elsewhere its setting
> And cometh from afar:
> Not in entire forgetfulness
> And not in utter nakedness,
> But trailing clouds of glory do we come
> From God, who is our home.

The next world is not situated on some distant planet, but is actually all around us in the very air that we breathe. Your loved one, whom you call dead, is carrying on his life right where you are now, but he is existing in his new body. You do not see him because he is now functioning in a body of vibrations too high for your mortal eye to register. You do not collide with him for the same reason that one radio program does not interfere with another. You and he are just on different wave lengths. Your body is dense; his body is etheric. Your mind is functioning on an alternating current; his mind is functioning on direct current. Death is just the change from one frequency or rate of vibration to another. It is the process of exchanging the lower speed for the higher; it makes no change in the real man at all. In fact, we shall be the same one minute after death as we were one minute before death except for appearance, and the difference is no more significant than the exchange of a winter suit for a summer one.

The effect of a change in frequency vibration (which is exactly what the transition from the mortal body to the spiritual body is) was brought out beautifully in Stewart Edward White's analysis of the movement of an electric fan. "Take the electric fan . . . a fan of two speeds. The low speed we'll label 50 and the high speed 100. We set the fan revolving at 50. It will go right on revolving at 50 indefinitely, though its over-all frequency is 100. In other words, without disturbing the potential of 100, we have arrested the fan's motion at 50.

"Now forgetting about 100 being a potential, we'll push the control level into high. With the fan going on twice as fast as before, we note a curious effect. . . . Whereas at 50 we could see the blades clearly, now we don't see them at all. We look right through them at the wall behind."

Paul said, *"We see as through a glass darkly,"* and Jesus said, *"If any man hath eyes to see, let him see."* The truth of the matter is that we see only that which is on our own level, or frequency. Fleshly bodies see only fleshly bodies, while spiritual bodies see only spiritual bodies. Just as you cannot see two sides of a coin at the same time, so you cannot see a spiritual body while you are still functioning in a physical body. To quote White again: "Did you ever see two sides of coin at one time? You could do that only with mirrors. Yet, seeing one side of a coin, you do not deny the existence of the other side, or that both sides belong to the same coin." And thus it is with death.

Death is but a change of frequency—a change from low visibility to high visibility. In this phase of life, as in every other, there can be no growth, progress, or unfoldment without change. This mortal body is dropped off so that the person who is said to be dying may assume another body suited to a new environment. We who are left behind no longer see the body (the blades) because the one who has made the change is now vibrating at a speed of 100, while we are still functioning at a speed of 50. Birth and death are two ends of the same thing. One is no more to be feared than the other, for each has purpose in God's plan.

As someone has wisely stated, "When we are in complete tune with the Infinite, we shall see the invisible. The whole atmosphere above us and all about us is full of life, full of the angels of God, full of ministering spirits, and our loved ones, walking unseen beside us. This is a universe of life, and not of death. You cannot destroy life. You can change its appearance and its relationships, but that is all that can be done. You can kill the body, but that will only release the soul into its true element—give it wings for flight into eternity."

Do you grieve because you no longer see your loved one? Then realize that the reason you do not see him is that the body he is now wearing is not visible to your physical eyes. He may be standing beside you right now in his spiritual body, but you in your physical body are unconscious of his presence.

"Will I ever see him?" you ask. Most certainly. "When?" When you go to sleep tonight. Sleep, you see, is a sort of temporary form of death. In fact, in many ways you will never be any more dead than when you go to sleep tonight. In natural sleep, all trace of personality is lost. You are "out," so to speak, and you enter into the same body as the one into which your loved one has passed. You are one with him in perfect consciousness, and your union with him is in every way as full as it used to be.

The only difference between those whom you call dead and those whom you call alive is a difference in consciousness and a difference in rate of vibration. The dead go to sleep in one room and wake up in another room; but you wake up in the same room. You will continue to wake up in the same room until the silver cord that keeps you and the natural body intact is broken. That which separates you finally from the physical body is the breaking of the silver cord; but until that time comes, you will continue to slip in and out of your physical body every twenty-four hours. When the cord is cut, your friends will call you dead, but actually you will be more alive than ever before.

"Behold I show you a mystery. We shall not all sleep." When man can bridge the gap between going to sleep and waking in the morning, he will never shed another tear, for he will then know what immortality is. When he can remember what happens during natural sleep, he will know that there are no dead. In the meantime, we shall not labor under the delusion that we have lost our dead, but shall realize that the only difference between them and us is that we are with them during the night while we are asleep and seem to be away from them during the day. In other words, death brings only a change of relationship, for it reverses the process of living. When we see death as an incident in life, we shall never think of our loved ones as being away from us. *"Lo, I am with you always."*

You ask, "What will be the nature of the life we are to live after death?" We can answer that it will be very similar to our present life. Eternal life is a present possession. It is the Christ-Life within us. The perfect will remain, and the imperfect, the un-Godlike, will pass away. It will be a spiritual life, as we shall abide in the home of the soul. We shall not be less human, but more really and ideally such. Three things we shall take with us from this life into the next: our thoughts, our feelings, our wills. What the character of that life shall be depends very largely upon what the character of our present life is.

Where are the dead? In the Father's House—Consciousness. We and the dead dwell in different rooms, in different states of consciousness. Morrison says: "It is all one house—it is all the Father's home—and we and the dead but dwell in different rooms. Not into any far country do we travel. . . . It is only a passing from one room to the other; a step through the veil into a brighter chamber." You would not weep if you could see things as they really are. Jesus said, *"I am come, that your joy may be full."* You look after a loved one with tear-dimmed eyes, but if you could follow that one into the glory of the *"temple not made with hands, eternal in the heavens,"* you would rejoice.

If you could see the things you think are causes for sorrow as God sees them, they would appear to be blessings. Someone has well said, "If Mary had found the body of Jesus in the tomb as she expected to do, it would have been a cause for grief. The empty tomb at which she grieved was the reason for the world's hope. Mary did not recognize Jesus. How needless her sorrow was!"

We often speak of our loved ones as though they were swept out of existence. It is difficult, in our hour of grief, to conceive that they have simply changed their relationship to us. We say of the sun at evening, "It has gone." Gone where? It has simply faded from our vision to shed its light on some other part of the globe. Our loved ones have simply gone to function in another state of consciousness and in another body, and to shine in another realm. Where is this other realm? Right where we are. *"In My Father's house are many mansions."* What tremendous power is expressed in these words! What radiant hope!

In an old and treasured sermon of an unknown source, the author asks and answers this question: "If energy can be transformed, but cannot be destroyed, then why should life — which is a form of energy — end at the change called death? If ether, so fine in texture as to be invisible, yet a substance, fills space and without break or puncture interpenetrates matter, then is it not conceivable that the soul after death inhabits a spiritual body in substance akin to ether and exists in a spiritual realm that interpenetrates our world?

"The words of Jesus, *'In My Father's house are many mansions,'* are descriptive of a spiritual realm no more mysterious than is life in our material world.

"The two worlds may not be far apart. Sugar dissolved in water is invisible. Yet it is there. Likewise the spiritual interpenetrates the material. Heaven is here all around us and it will be to us here and hereafter just exactly what we are to it."

Your dead are near to you, rest assured. That the two planes of activity on which the living and the so-called dead function may be superimposed is readily within our comprehension. Surely, when we live our lives surrounded by the mysteries of creation, when we depend upon natural laws for our movements and our sustenance, the acceptance of the knowledge of the continuity of life should not be difficult.

JOURNEY'S END

("The spirit shall return to God who gave it.")

We go from God to God — then though
    The way be long,
We shall return to Heaven, our home,
    At evensong.

We go from God to God — so let
    The space between
Be filled with beauty, conquering
    Things base and mean.

We go from God to God — lo! what
    Transcendent bliss
To know the journey's end will hold
    Such joy as this.

EVELYN HEALEY

CHAPTER 8

Two Bodies

*"THERE IS A NATURAL BODY AND
THERE IS A SPIRITUAL BODY."*

What we name death is merely changing one suit of clothes or one dress for another. In our physical lives, new garments to replace the old and worn-out are occasions for rejoicing. Then what are you grieving about? That is a pertinent question, and one which every sorrowing person must face. You have not lost the one whom you call dead because you no longer see the garment to which you were accustomed. The garment has been cast aside, but the one who wore it is very much alive. Does this mean then that the physical body is unimportant? No. But it means that it belongs to the material plane only. God has provided a finer body for a higher plane — *"An house not made with hands, eternal in the heavens."*

"No man hath seen God at any time; the only begotten Son . . . he hath declared him." You have never really seen your loved one any more than you

have ever seen life or spirit. You have known only the house in which he lived. Is it so hard then to believe in the real self or spiritual body of your loved one? Doesn't the natural body prove the reality of the spiritual? Doesn't the effect reveal the cause? Aren't we all incarnations of God?

"There is a natural body and there is a spiritual body," or we might say that there is a human body and there is a Christ-Body. Please notice the tense of this statement. The word *is* means that you possess both of these bodies right now; it means that they are not successive. Yes, you who read these lines have both a human body that is visible and an inner Christ-Body that is invisible. When you lay aside the human, or natural body, you still have that other finer, spiritual, Christ-Body.

To understand this analogy, you must realize that there is a vast difference between the body of Jesus and the Body of Christ. The body of Jesus was the natural body which was sacrificed on the cross. The body of Christ is the spiritual body, *"an house not made with hands, eternal in the heavens."* The Christ-Body has always been coexistent with God; it was formed in the image and likeness of God and is the perfect idea of man. It was of this Body that Jesus said, *"Lo, I am with you always."* Since the

Body of Christ is spiritual, it is likewise omnipresent. Yes, your loved one is with you constantly, for St. Paul said, *"Now ye are the Body of Christ, and members in particular."* The human body is but the temple of the Real Man who is One with the Father. Being Spiritual, this body is One in All and All in One, and knows no separation of any kind except in human belief. This realization of Oneness will do away with all grief and sorrow, for in this knowledge, *"He shall wipe away all tears."*

If you stand before a mirror, you see a body which is composed of liquids, solids, and gases; but back of that body and interpenetrating it is another and even more substantial Body which you do not see. The natural body has been likened to a man's overcoat and the Spiritual Body to the ordinary suit coat worn underneath the overcoat. Hold that for a moment, and you will see that the Resurrection Body is already in existence.

When a man falls asleep (dies) on this plane, he wakes up on the other plane with his Resurrection Body functioning in place of the physical body he left behind. In other words, he leaves one body to occupy another.

How then does personality survive death? Because

the Spiritual Body which we take with us is the re-
pository of our character, thoughts, and feelings.
We take these with us; all else is left behind. Death
to the egg means birth to the chick. Death to the
seed means birth to the plant. Death to the old
means birth to the new. The whole impetus of creation is charged with the words: "Go forward. You
cannot stay in any one place too long. If you do,
you will retrogress. You will become fixed, inflexi-
ble, and solid. Change is inevitable, and it is good."

"Behold, I make all things new." Death is but
another side to life. Matter and Spirit are two
aspects of one thing. A shield may be gold on one
side and silver on the other; but you cannot see both
sides at once, nor can you describe one side by looking at the other side. If you want to picture the
shield completely, you must have two pictures and
not one, but the shield is one, nevertheless.

Death is a gap in consciousness. Within the old
body is the new body. Within the old heaven is the
new heaven. Within the old earth is the new earth.
The Eternal Body is within the temporal body.

"In all probability, there is a body within a body
to infinity," says Ernest Holmes. He continues: "We
do not depart from reason when we assume this, for

while we say that two bodies cannot occupy the same space simultaneously, we must remember that we are talking about only one plane of expression. . . . The new idea of matter and ether has proved that form can lie within form without interference, for it has been shown conclusively that there is a substance which can occupy the same space which our body does."

The truth of the matter is that man departs this body only to find himself equipped with another one. He carries with him every attribute that he now possesses, and goes forth in complete retention of his individuality. He simply dies from the physical plane to the spiritual plane; from the physical body to the spiritual body. Life does not end for a single moment. It merely changes form and condition. *"In my Father's house are many mansions"*— planes of consciousness; each one is keyed to a different vibration and degree of life.

"I am the resurrection and the life." I AM— present tense. *I AM* right now in the midst of a life for which there is no death. Do you think of your departed loved one as a physical body or as an immortal soul? Do you think of him as an individualization of the principle of life or as a material man who was destined to die? There is a vast difference, you see, between physicality and Individuality. The

materialist sums up life by saying, "Change and de-cay in all around I see." The spiritual man sums up life by saying, "O Thou who changest not, abide with me." What a comforting thought that is! It reveals the possibility of living Eternal Life here and now. When you say *I AM*, you are individualizing the Principle of Life. You are declaring your indis-soluble union with God. You are talking about that part of your being which is not subject to death. It is the Principle of Identity that was never born, never gets sick, and never dies.

Is this hard for you to understand? Then let us use another illustration. When you individualize the principle of mathematics, you say 2x2 = 4. Can there be death for that fact? Can 2x2 ever become five, six, or anything else? Can the principle ever die? Can it ever change? To be sure, the crayons, pencils, and paper that you use to figure it are perishable, but the formula itself moves in a sphere in which death is unknown. The fact, *two times two are four,* is an individualization of the principle of mathematics which is eternal. The answer will al-ways be *four;* it can never be anything else. So it is with the individuality of man.

Jesus said, *"Before Abraham was, I am."* Before my physical body appeared on this plane, I was. Af-ter my physical body disappears from this plane, I shall be. From the Universal standpoint, I AM means God; from the individual standpoint, I AM means the spiritual self. The I AM in you is the life of you, and without this I AM you could not be. You can cut out a man's appendix, his kidney, his gall bladder. You can take off an arm, a foot, or a leg, but he goes right on saying, "I AM; I AM; I do; I think; I will; I say." The I AM in man, you see, is God — that beside which there is no other. It is the one thing about him that can never be cut out, taken out, or reasoned out. The I AM of man is permanent, fixed, and true. It is an individualization of the Principle of Life.

"I am God, and there is none else." The principle of identity holds in every realm of nature and on every plane of life. One of the most beautiful illustrations of this principle is the life-cycle of the butterfly. It moves unerringly through the egg-worm-chrysalis stages to bring to life the triumphant and beautiful winged creature that so delights us. When you hold the lowly acorn in your hand, you are holding not only an acorn but also potential tons and tons of timber. The acorn itself weighs just a fraction of an ounce, but when it falls into the earth and dies, it produces a great tree.

Death is as truly a step forward in a life's history as is birth. As we make the change from the natural body to the spiritual body, we become invisible to those who knew us only after the flesh; and we become visible to those who know us only after the spirit because they are manifesting themselves in the same kind of body. We are, in this experience, like the vine that grows up by the side of the fence and passes up over the top to bloom; the flower of life (Individuality) is on the other side.

Do you walk toward your tomb with mighty interrogations leaping from your lips, or do you face it calmly and unafraid because you know that it is empty? *"Why weepest thou? Whom seekest thou?"* *"Why seek ye the living among the dead?"* *"He is not here but is risen."* Your loved one is closer to you now than ever before. Would you put him away from you by your belief that he is dead? Or, rather, will you say with the Shunammite woman of long ago, *"IT IS WELL"*?

AFTER DEATH IN ARABIA

Faithful friends! It lies I know
Pale and white and cold as snow:
And ye say, "Abdallah's dead!"
Weeping at the feet and head.
I can see your falling tears,
I can hear your sighs and prayers.
Yet I smile and whisper this:
"I am not the thing you kiss.
Cease your tears, and let it lie.
It was mine — It is not I."

SIR EDWIN ARNOLD

CHAPTER 9

Sudden Death

"IN THE MIDST OF LIFE, WE ARE IN DEATH."

If one wants to know about sudden and tragic death, all he has to do is to pick up one of the daily newspapers. An airplane engine fails, and fifty or sixty lives are snuffed out. Hotels, hospitals, homes, and theaters burn, and hundreds are cremated. Automobiles come together on the highways, and whole families are wiped out. Rivers go on a rampage, and thousands are drowned. Millions are killed in war, and other millions starve to death from famines in distant lands.

"How terrible!" we say when we read of a tragedy. But since we do not know the persons involved and we face no visible evidence, our emotion, though sincere, tends to be fleeting. When tragedy strikes our next-door neighbor, our sympathies are much more involved and usually result in action, but we still tend to feel that we are immune. Such things may happen to others, but surely sudden death has no place in the pattern of our lives.

Then with the suddenness of an earthquake or an explosion, everything in our world comes to a stop. A dear friend or relative is unexpectedly snatched from our lives. This crushing blow disarranges our life, nullifies our plans, scatters our hopes, and shatters our faith. We cry out: "Why did this have to happen to me? What have I done that God should send such a terrible thing into my life?"

It is difficult to answer questions of this nature to the comfort of those who are suffering from the shock of sudden loss because they are not rational at such a time. The difficulty is increased because of the lack of preparation for the grief that has come. We need to learn the truth in the statement: "In the midst of life, we are in death." Those words were not written for the few who seem destined for violent or untimely death, but for all of us. They were written not to ease our sorrow, but to prepare us for the inevitable separations which are bound to come. The price we pay at such a time is always determined by the spiritual resources at our command. We rise or fall according to the scope of our faith, the depth of our poise, and the measure of our self-control.

Unless we still think of God as an arbitrary and vindictive power who sends destruction and misery upon some and happiness and peace upon others, we cannot blame Him when tragedy strikes. If He does not know both good and evil, as Habakkuk says, how can He send sickness and affliction as a punishment for sin? Physical health is governed by physical laws. When these laws are broken, man becomes sick. Just as financial collapse is the result of failure to cooperate with economic laws, physical collapse is the result of failure to observe the laws governing physical health. In other words, there is no punishment for the breaking of a law, but there is an inevitable consequence.

It is not God's Will that anyone should be mutilated by accident or broken by disease. *"I am come that ye might have life and have it more abundantly."* It is His Will that we continue in the physical body in perfect health until our life work is done and the organs of the body wear out. God doesn't arbitrarily call us home before our time or send affliction to punish us for our misdeeds. God is Love. God is Life. God is Law. God is Truth. God is Good.

St. Matthew said: *"Ye know neither the day nor the hour wherein the Son of man cometh."* Many people regard sudden death with revulsion and dread. To the survivors, it is a crushing blow. To the departed, it is a relief and blessing. The way in which we go or the time at which we go is not the important thing. The supremely important thing is our readiness to make the change, and over this we have control. Readiness is a matter of being reconciled and prepared, of living each day as though it were our last, of being prepared for the sudden termination of earthly ties. Death is lamentable only when there are unfinished tasks, unquenched anger, poisonous grudges, unreconciled enmities, and unhealed wounds. It is too late when death strikes to make things right. Everyone should square his accounts every day.

Deathbed repentance is probably better than no repentance at all; but repentance means a change of mind and heart, and change takes time, for it is a matter of behavior, character, discipline, and consciousness. It is a way of life.

No one in his right mind is going to choose sudden death over natural death, but it does have many compensations. Think of the many sorrows, heartaches, and perplexities the departed loved one has been spared. Think of the difference between the clean dispatch of sudden death as compared with the painful, slow disintegration of the body which marks the approach of death for many and particularly for the aged. Death is the same whether it comes quickly or slowly.

Our thoughts about death, like many of our funeral customs, are pagan. After two thousand years of Christian teaching and faith, we still talk about broken circles and splintered columns. Death is not the end of something but the beginning of something, whether it approaches gradually or suddenly. We can not go into eternity, for we are already in it. The dead are no more in eternity now than they always were, or than every one of us is at this moment. Despite its two aspects, there is only one Life and that Life is here and now.

The Bible does not tell us very much about the life after death, but it does assure us of the continuity of consciousness and personality. We shall know each other as we are known. That fact was brought out in Jesus' statement to the thief on the cross: *"This day thou shalt be with me in Paradise.* [Right now our bodies are stretched between earth and sky in crucifixion, but in a little while we shall be united on another plane.]"

In both the Old and New Testaments, there are many assurances of our recognition of one another in the next life. None is more significant than this one: *"Abraham . . . died in a good old age, . . . and was gathered unto his people, . . . and his sons buried him."* Analyze that statement carefully, and you will see that the reunion with his people (*"was gathered unto his people"*) comes before the burial of his body.

We find this same thought expressed in the command of the Lord to Moses: *"Get thee up into this mountain Abarim, unto Mount Nebo, . . . and die in the mount whither thou goest up, and be gathered unto thy people; as Aaron thy brother died in Mount Hor, and was gathered unto his people."* What is God promising Moses in this command? He is promising him that when he dies on Mount Nebo, he will be united with his loved ones on the spiritual plane. David brought out this same idea in his sorrow at the death of his child: *"I shall go to him, but he shall not return to me."*

Life does not end in the grave: it only seems to end in the family circle. It makes no difference whether death comes quickly or slowly. The result is the same. Death is swallowed up in victory. The dead and the living are different rooms in the Father's House — yet not divided.

DEATH IS A DOOR

Death is only an old door
    Set in a garden wall.
On gentle hinges it gives at dusk,
When the thrushes call.

Along the lintel are green leaves;
    Beyond, the light lies still.
Very willing and weary feet
    Go over that sill.

There is nothing to trouble any heart,
    Nothing to hurt at all.
Death is only a quiet door
    In an old wall.

NANCY BYRD TURNER

CHAPTER 10

How to Meet Sorrow

*"LET NOT YOUR HEART BE TROUBLED,
NEITHER LET IT BE FEARFUL."*

Anything as devastating and destructive as grief must be handled with intelligence, understanding, and wisdom. It cannot be avoided, denied, delayed, suppressed, or ignored. It must be met; it must be analyzed. The true cause must be determined. To run away or to hide from grief results in the need to meet it at some future time in a more terrible form. The metaphysician says that grief has been met only when it has been faced. Jesus said, *"Agree with thine adversary quickly, whiles thou art in the way with him."* In other words, face your grief and rob it of its power. See it for what it is, and it will cease to trouble you. When you accept the worst, the wound it has made begins to heal.

"But that is not according to the teachings of my church," you may say. "Why should I grieve when I believe that death is the gateway to a beautiful and more wonderful life?" If your belief in immortality is sufficient to heal your sense of separation, this treatise is not for you. You should make sure, however, that you are not deluding yourself. The knowledge that our loved ones are alive in another sphere of activity does not by itself compensate for the sense of loss and emptiness which we feel on the relative plane.

"There is a natural body and there is a spiritual body." It is the death of the natural body that has caused your grief. Yesterday, you could see your loved one, talk with him, and caress him. Today, his body is cold and still. The tenant has gone; nothing remains but an empty shell. If this is your conclusion, it is apparent that you have been confusing spiritual life with mortal life. In our present state of consciousness, the agreement with death must be both physical and spiritual. View it as you will, the departure of a loved one leaves an emptiness on the physical plane that must be filled.

If you sincerely believe that your loved one is dead only in the flesh, you can further help him and yourself by giving no outward denial of that belief and by making your period of mourning as brief as possible. In order to assist you in overcoming grief, I have prepared a series of steps for you to follow. These steps will not be easy for you in the beginning, but you owe it to your loved one and to yourself to make a conscious effort to overcome your grief. He has earned the rest and happiness that have now come to him. Since you would not willingly hamper him in his onward way, you must not give way to self-pity.

STEP 1. FACE YOUR GRIEF

The first step in overcoming your grief is to face it. In the beginning, there may be great shock, bewilderment, numbness, and sadness. The light seemingly has gone out, and you are left in darkness. Your life has been emptied by loneliness and sorrow; you wonder how you can go on. You had no idea that you could ever be so distraught and forlorn. Living without your loved one is too terrible to contemplate. Then comes a bitter period of tears and sobbing. Do not try to repress or suppress it. The expression of grief is part of the cure and not a sign of weakness. *"Jesus wept."* He was not ashamed of His weeping. If you do not really feel like crying, try to cry anyway. Tears help to remove the tension of sorrow. This tendency to weep may go on for several days; but it will soon spend itself, and you will feel relieved. Talk about the deceased in great detail. Recall all the memories of your associations with him. Review all the circumstances of his last illness. Tell what his death means to you. In other words, talk him out of yourself. It will help to release the tension and to heal the pain.

Grief, however, is a luxury. It is one of the most expensive of all emotions. It costs more physically and mentally than almost any other mood. Carried to excess, it works great injury and harm to the deceased and produces great loss in the body and affairs of the bereaved. Grief changes the secretions, slows down the circulation, weakens the tissues, and depresses the nerves.

If you mourn excessively for the loved one who has made the change, if you prolong your sorrow, grief, gloom, and depression, you not only widen your sense of separation, but you wrap yourself round with a heavy cloud that darkens the upward way of your loved one. Even though he is no longer attached to you physically, his great love and sympathy for you cause him to suffer witih your suffering and to grieve with your grieving. What you need to remember at such a time is that your loved one does not die until you forget him or drop him out of your consciousness. He has never in reality existed anywhere but in consciousness; as long as your awareness of him lives, he never dies to you. Life is a state of consciousness. It knows no interruption, separation, or cessation. The past is linked to the present; the future is formed in the NOW. In this sense, your loved one can never die, for he lives on in the minds and lives of those left behind. He is not far or near, according to physical presence or absence; it is not a question of *hereness or thereness.*

According to Ernest Wilson, "We are close to those who are dear to us because they are dear to us, because we have much in common, because our attachment to them is not an attachment of the body but of the mind and the Spirit. We sense that nearness when our letters cross in the mail and answer questions before they are received and when, without outward means of communication, we are subtly aware of one another's deep thoughts and feelings.

"We are near to others in proportion to the things that we have in common with them. It is thus that we may be near, in Spirit, to those who are out of the body.

"It is natural for us to like to have near to us those that we love, but just as we are willing to let them leave us to go away to school, or to take up some new work, or for some other good reason, so too we should not seek to bind to us those who slip out of the body. We should love them unselfishly enough to free them from our personal will or desire. We should bless them with our realization that they are safely held in the love and wisdom of God, and that He leads them step by step into that which is for their highest good."

It is, of course, difficult to tell you not to grieve when someone whom you love dearly has passed from your sight, but the fact remains that grief is definitely harmful, both to your loved one and to you.

"The attitude of grief," Christian D. Larson says, "wastes the tissues both in the body and in the brain. The thought of grief is loss, and, as like causes like, the thought of grief will naturally produce loss wherever it may act: that is, it will cause the tissues to waste away and will cause the system to lose much of its life and energy. Those who have grieved much have felt this loss among the elements of their own system, and, when we look at those who grieve, we discover the wasting process at work in every fibre. Nothing is gained but much is lost through grief."

STEP 2. DISABUSE YOUR MIND OF ALL SENSE OF GUILT

One of the things that intensify the pain of sorrow is the actual or imagined neglect of the deceased. "If only I had bought that house my wife wanted, it would have given her so much happiness." "If only I had taken Bill to the doctor sooner, he would have been alive today." "If only I had called a specialist." "If only I had gone to the store myself, instead of sending Mary." "If only I had done this or that." People who encourage such thoughts not only tend to be irrational and morbid, but are bent on their own destruction.

"To err is human; to forgive divine." In an unfinished world like ours, mistakes are bound to occur, but they should not result in self-torture. If a tragedy is caused by your own conscious, wilful, wrong action, the hardest part of your present task is to face the fact and forgive yourself even as you know your loved one has forgiven you. It is, of course, too late to do the things you might have done for him, but your duty now is to the living. What has been left undone cannot be done, and when you face that fact, you are ready to rebuild. We are all likely in the shock of our loss to feel a sense of guilt for things left undone, or done too quickly, or done in the wrong way. More often than not, our memory of these acts or incidents is distorted. The guilt we feel may have little or no cause in reality.

It is important, therefore, that you rationalize this sense of guilt and forgive yourself as quickly as possible. Then you must take time to do the thing that should be done to crowd out the grief. Perhaps one of your difficulties lies in the fact that you do not take time to live. We must all learn that a better tomorrow is determined not by what we plan for the future, but by what we do today.

Did it ever occur to you to wonder why that better tomorrow never comes? It is because we do not do what we ought to do today. *"Carpe diem."* Remorse is difficult to meet and overcome; the way to prevent it is to do today what ought to be done.

In England, there is an old sundial that carries this inscription: "It is later than you think." Meditate upon that for a moment. It means that today may be the only day you will ever have. If you are waiting for your ship to come in, you might better go home and forget it. Jesus said, *"Take no thought for the morrow."* The morrow never comes because it is always today. If you are planning some happiness for the future, face the fact that you may never realize it. The only things that can be done must be done NOW.

Time and opportunities lost today cannot be recovered tomorrow. If you would avoid regrets, do now the things that ought to be done. "It is later than you think." Sit down and make a list of those relatives and friends whom you are neglecting. When you have an impulse to say or do something nice for a member of your family, a relative, or a friend, do it at once. If something pleases you, speak about it. If you have appreciation, voice it. "It is later than you think." A man cannot smell flowers when he is dead. Live each day as though it were the first and last day you will ever have. Do the things you can do and ought to do now.

STEP 3. GET A SPIRITUAL RELATIONSHIP WITH YOUR LOVED ONE

After you have realistically faced your feeling of guilt, the next step is to get a more spiritual relationship with your loved one — to see and know him as he is. You must renew old friendships and cultivate new ones, but no one, of course, can ever take the place of the one that has gone. Only a spiritual relationship can do that. If you identify your loved one with the physical body, you will never bridge the gap. The body is not the self of your loved one. He is not his body. He is not his mind. He has a body and he has a mind, but he is Spirit. He is a son of God.

"The Spirit itself beareth witness with our spirit, that we are children of God: and if children, then heirs; heirs of God, and joint heirs with Christ."

"God Himself shall be with them, and be their God. And God shall wipe away all tears from their eyes; and there shall be no more death, neither sorrow, nor crying, neither shall there be any more pain: for the former things are passed away."

Can you imagine anything worse than living forever in your present body subject as it is to so many ills and to so much suffering? If death were the end of life, there might be some cause for your grief. The body is one of God's greatest gifts to man; it makes him visible to others. It has but one purpose — to connect the individual with the outer, or physical plane of being. But the self of man does not die when the body is laid aside any more than your life is over when you cast off an old suit of clothes.

"Why seek ye the living among the dead?" Why seek to identify your loved one with an old suit of clothes? *"He is not here, but is risen."* A dead body

is no more sacred than an old coat, suit, or dress with which you have finished. It is merely an aggregation of atoms and molecules of such elements as iron, phosphorous, silica, carbon, nitrogen, lime, and water for which your loved one has no further use; it should be disposed of with the utmost cleanliness and reverence as quickly as possible.

Your loved one has already worn out and disposed of many physical bodies by the natural process of replacement, and the body which you now call dead is the last one. But it was the man, woman, or child that you loved, and not the body, just as it is the living individual you love and not the blue suit or the red dress that is worn. That which made the body precious and important to you was the light of the soul which shone through it.

Now ask yourself, "What am I grieving over?" Is it the man that you loved, or the chemical aggregation that you call his body? Do eyes see? Do ears hear? Do brains think? Do lips speak? No; if they did, they would go on seeing, hearing, thinking, and speaking forever. We leave these organs behind. The inner self uses them as a violinist uses his violin. Can a violin produce music apart from the human hand? Is the human body of any value apart from the invisible Spirit that uses it? Don't you see that the soul simply discards the old body when it puts on a new one just as you discard an old worn-out garment?

Myron Lee Pontius says, "To cling lovingly to the shells that we have known, to lavish upon them our affection, to identify them with our beloved, is perfectly natural — natural, but not spiritual; it savors of a materialistic disbelief in the survival of individuality apart from the body.

"You are interested in your home and if it should be destroyed you would grieve because of the loss of the house and the loss of many valuable and personal possessions which are considered priceless. But if you should move from the home, taking with you all the treasured possessions and then discover that the house had been destroyed, you would not experience so much disappointment. The body of your beloved dead is the house in which he lived and that body will be completely destroyed after a few passing years. He has taken all his valued possessions, including character and memory, and entered into 'an house not made with hands.' We should give more attention to the life of the departed, remembering the things that are spiritual and abiding, and we should give much less attention to the house of clay and a much less expenditure of time and money in caring for the abandoned house in which our loved one lived while in this world."

STEP 4. KEEP YOUR POISE

If there is any time in which a person needs to keep his poise and to be guided by reason, it is when he is under the spell of grief. Why do we say this? Because of the tendency of grief-stricken persons to lavish money upon the dead body out of all proportion to its importance. They forget that the body is a cast-off garment; and forgetting, they are tempted to spend money on funerals and expensive formalities which they honestly cannot afford.

It is wise to keep the burial services as simple, dignified, and beautiful as possible and always within the financial ability of the family to pay. Many of our funeral customs today are purely pagan. They not only add to the mourner's grief, but place financial obligations on him which are hard to meet. The deceased is adorned in material finery which he had never known on earth. He is placed in an expensive casket, and people file past to stare at the deserted house. Is that kindness to the deceased? Opening the casket only serves to identify the self of the deceased with the house of clay. There is no benefit in an expensive funeral except to the undertaker. The memory of it soon vanishes, and the satisfaction of the survivors is spoiled by the binding debt that must be paid.

Another pagan practice of our time is the custom of moving bodies from one city or town to another. What difference does it make where the dust rests? Is one place better than another? Is the earth in Philadelphia any more sacred than the earth in Denver, or Los Angeles? Does it make any difference to the insensate body where it is buried?

The sane and sanitary way to dispose of the cast-off body is to send it quickly back to its source through the purifying power of flames.

The author prophesies a time when all funeral services will be private and without ostentation or show. Sorrow is a very personal and intimate thing. The burial service should be a very simple and inspiring ceremony, preferably held in the church, with just the minister, family, and intimate friends present. This plan would not only eliminate much morbid grief and pain but also many of the needless and numberless formalities that have grown up in recent years.

Another important factor in preparing for the inevitable is to select an undertaker before the final summons comes. The funeral director performs an important and vital service to every family; he should be a man who has your utmost confidence, esteem, respect, and trust. Most funeral directors are conscientious, capable, and reliable. A few are unethical and commercial. You can avoid the latter by carefully selecting the right one before death comes. It will not only lighten the burden of your sorrow, but give you a sense of confidence, satisfaction, and peace.

STEP 5. COMMUNE WITH YOUR DEPARTED IN CONSCIOUSNESS

If you believe in immortality as Jesus taught and demonstrated it, you know that your loved one is not in the cemetery. You should keep away from it; seek your loved one in consciousness, for Life is a state of consciousness which is the same on both sides of the grave. If you desire to keep the memory of your loved one fresh by remembering his anniversaries, commemorate his birthdays and not his death. Send flowers to the altar or sanctuary of your church; appropriate prayers will be said, and you will come into closer fellowship with him. To be close to your loved ones in the Spiritual Body, you must be close to God.

If there is only One Mind in which we eternally dwell, there is nothing to sever our communication with the departed but our belief that they are dead.

Archdeacon Wilberforce brought out this idea in his conception of Holy Communion as a trysting place for the visible and the invisible. He said: "As every telephone in this great city opens communication with another telephone common to both, so do sundered souls, though between them lies all the inexplicable mystery of another world, find each other in the presence and in the heart of a Savior common to both. We cannot see them in that other dimension of space, neither could we see them if they were at the antipodes; but whenever we draw near to the heart of the Risen Lord, we draw near also to those who are in the world of Spirits."

STEP 6. AVOID THE APPEARANCE OF SORROW

The next step in meeting sorrow is to avoid the appearance of sorrow. If you believe that life is eternal, one of the greatest injustices you can do your loved one is to drape yourself in black raiment, black armlets, and black ties. *"In Him was life; and the life was the light of men."* The true funeral color is white, according to the New Testament. White is the composite of all the other colors. Black is dead, lifeless, and depressing. It has no vibration and always smacks of superstition. Wearing a mourning veil originally was for the purpose of protection against the vengeance of the dead. Once it was the custom to open the window so that the spirit of the dying person might escape the walls of the house and to close it again to keep the spirit from re-entering. The second practice is recognized as pure superstition, but the first one has established itself as a custom.

Jesus' tomb on the resurrection morning was flooded with light, a dazzling white light, and the young man standing there was arrayed in white. White shows forth the nothingness of death, while black is a denial of everything that Jesus taught. There is no night (darkness) in the City Foursquare.

Crushing though our suffering be, we have no right to parade our sorrow before others. "We have no right," someone has said, "to cast gloom over happy natures by our weight of crepe, by serving the term prescribed for wearing the livery of mourning, as if grief thought of wearing a uniform. We have no right to syndicate our grief by using note paper with a heavy black border as wide as a hat band, thus parading our sorrow to others in their happiest moments."

All the water in the world cannot sink a ship unless it gets inside the ship. All the sorrow in the world cannot hurt you unless it gets inside your mind. Thoughts form, as it were, an atmosphere through which every external event must pass. They are the real things from whence all joy, from whence all sorrow springs.

STEP 7. BUSY YOURSELF IN SOME USEFUL AND ABSORBING OCCUPATION

One of the quickest ways to overcome sorrow and sadness is to undertake some useful and absorbing work for others. You forget by serving. It is natural to grieve when a dear one has departed, but it is not the way to show love for those who have slipped out of our life. Sorrow benefits neither the bereaved nor the deceased. When you realize that your grief is for yourself and not for him, you have taken from bereavement its greatest power to hurt and pain you. Your duty now is to the living, and you should occupy yourself with some useful activity that will help you to forget. Instead of tearing yourself to pieces over the dead, you should be working enthusiastically to improve the conditions of the living. You can do this through your church or through some welfare organization. The world is full of half-starved and under-privileged children who need your help.

Then there are the many societies and organizations for the prevention of cruelty to animals. The question of vivisection is stirring people from coast to coast. By joining an Anti-Vivisection Society, you can help to bring these hideous tortures and horrible sacrifices to an end. The good vivisection does is not at all in proportion to the suffering it causes.

More profitable than grieving for the departed is making life a noble testimony to our love for them.

* * * *

I take leave of you for the moment, confident that, in the light of these truths, you will meet your sorrow with a calm and even mind. I am asking God to reveal this mystery to you, and through these words, to wipe away all tears from your eyes. Armed with true understanding you have nothing to fear, either in life or in death. God is in both, and where God is, there is no lack. Your loved one is alive, more alive than ever before. He is going to live forever. You are going to live forever. "The best is yet to be." The future will always be better than the present or the past, for you are ever growing and progressing, and you are an immortal soul.

I want you to feel the substance, the life, the comfort, and the love that come to you in this blessing. As I send it forth, it is as though the Kingdom of God were opened; I feel a great wave of the Father's rich love encompassing all the earth in lasting peace and understanding. God bless you!

Robert A. Russell

ACKNOWLEDGMENTS

Any author finds himself under obligation to many persons who do not receive formal credit. There are those to whom he is indebted for ideas; and there are others whose words are remembered when their source is forgotten or impossible to identify. The appreciation of the author is no less sincere because of the impossibility of publicly recognizing their individual assistance.

In the brief bibliography that follows, the author wishes to acknowledge with deep gratitude his use of specific quotations of some length.

CHAPTER 1. A LETTER

Gilkey, James Gordon. *When Life Gets Hard.* The Macmillan Company.
Greer, Ina May. "Grief Must Be Faced." *The Christian Century.* Feb. 28, 1945.

CHAPTER 2. GRIEF

Crowell, Grace Noll. "They Shall Be Comforted." Taken from *Songs for Courage.* Harper & Row.

CHAPTER 3. THIS IS ETERNAL LIFE

Holmes, Ernest. *This Thing Called Life*. G. P. Putnam's Sons.

Dunnington, Lewis L. *Handles of Power*. Abingdon-Cokesbury Press.

Cook, Jay. *Lessons in the Absolute*. Used by permission of Carrick-Cook.

Boone, J. Allen. *Letters to Strongheart*. Prentice-Hall, Inc.

Pardue, Austin. *He Lives*. Morehouse-Gorham Co., New York.

CHAPTER 4. THE DEAD ARE THE LIVING

Cook, Jay. *Lessons in the Absolute*. Used by permission of Carrick-Cook.

Williams, Vivian May. *There Is Nothing But God*. DeVorss & Co.

CHAPTER 5. THE FRIENDLY ENEMY

Collier, Robert. *Be Rich*. Used by permission.

Boone, J. Allen. *Letters to Strongheart*. Prentice-Hall, Inc.

Worcester, Elwood. *Making Life Better*. Charles Scribner's Sons.

Foley, Virginia. "They Called Him Death." *100 Poems of Immortality*. Thomas C. Clark.

CHAPTER 7. WHERE ARE THE DEAD?

White, Stewart Edward. *The Unobstructed Universe*. E. P. Dutton and Company.

Healey, Evelyn. "Journey's End." *100 Poems of Immortality*. Thomas C. Clark.

CHAPTER 8. TWO BODIES

Holmes, Ernest. *The Science of Mind*. G. P. Putnam's Sons.

Arnold, Edwin. "After Death in Arabia." From *Pearls of the Faith*. Little, Brown & Co.

CHAPTER 9. SUDDEN DEATH

Turner, Nancy Byrd. "Death Is a Door." *100 Poems of Immortality*. Thomas C. Clark.

CHAPTER 10. HOW TO MEET SORROW

Wilson, Ernest G. *Unity Monthly.* Unity School of Christianity.

Larson, Christian D. *How to Stay Well.* Used by permission of the author.

Pontius, Myron Lee. *When Sorrow Comes.* Used by permission of the author.